S0-FAH-319

A Call to
PRAYER

Inspirational Prayer from the Bible

to Jennifer
with all the
great love of
Christ

J Joey

Jer 29:12
v. 9-12

JORDANIS JOSEPH

A CALL TO PRAYER
Copyright © 2018 by Jordanis Joseph

All rights reserved. Neither this publication nor any part of this publication may be reproduced or transmitted in any form or by any means, electronic or mechanical, including photocopying, recording or any information storage and retrieval system, without permission in writing from the author.

The views and opinions expressed in this publication belong solely to the author, and do not reflect those of Word Alive Press or any of its employees.

Unless otherwise indicates, scripture taken from the New King James Version®. Copyright © 1982 by Thomas Nelson. Used by permission. All rights reserved. Scriptures marked (KJV) taken from the Holy Bible, which is in the public domain.

Printed in Canada

ISBN: 978-1-4866-1647-3

Word Alive Press
119 De Baets Street, Winnipeg, MB R2J 3R9
www.wordalivepress.ca

Cataloguing in Publication may be obtained through Library and Archives Canada

Contents

Acknowledgements

My thanks go, first of all, to God, our Father in heaven who listens to and answers prayers, to Jesus Christ our Lord, our Saviour who teaches us how to pray, and commands us to do so always, and to the Holy Spirit, our Helper who always intervenes when we don't know what we should pray for as we ought, and intercedes for us in language above human understanding.

To my wife and our children, who sustained and encouraged me through their prayers all along this wonderful journey, and a special thanks to my daughter Rebecca, for her constant assistance, technical support, and advice. To my father Minister Josema Joseph, my first example of a man of prayer.

To God be all the glory!

Preface

Inspirational Prayer from the Bible does not intend to be a collection of prayers chosen here and there from different books of the Bible. Neither is it meant to be a list of them. Instead it will be at the same time an invitation to pray more and an appeal to see prayer through the same eyes and spirit which the elders of the faith—men and women of God in the Bible—saw it when they faced their own situations in moments of great need, and during their times of intimate fellowship with the Lord.

As believers, we are called to pray in the same manner as those giants of the faith, remarkable servants of the Lord whose testimonies have been given to us as examples throughout the Bible. Because their prayers attracted the attention of God, bringing prodigious results, let us have a look on them and understand how much the Spirit of God guided them, helping them to address to God the kind of prayers that are so pleasant to Him. By doing so, we can be inspired for our own approach to God today. May we be led by the Holy Spirit, and receive directions and inspiration for our prayer life. My prayer is that it will be so for you in Jesus' name!

About Prayer

Prayer, the singular act which is discussed in this book, is one of the most familiar spiritual acts or gestures in a believer's life, besides reading the Bible, meditating on the Word of God, fasting, singing, praising, worshiping, dancing before the Lord, and so on.

Prayer opens the way for dialogue between us and heaven. It not only gives us the privilege to address God anytime, anywhere, but it also grants us the right to intercede on behalf of others, countries, leaders, and people in authority. It enables us to command, to open prison doors, to intervene in times of disaster, to set captives free, to establish, to create, and to reverse. Through prayer, we confidently submit our burden to God and relax ourselves in the Lord's precious arms, in the sweetness of His company. We pour out our souls in prayer before the Lord in times of sorrow, and at the same time, through prayer, we find comfort and peace.

Through prayer, by faith, we can stand confidently in front of trials, difficulties, and adversaries; we can stand particularly strong when our prayer is fed with the living Word of God. That's why true prayer and the Word of God always go together. We pray that the Holy Spirit will open the eyes of our understanding so that we will see what God wants to say. The Word of God, penetrating our soul, spirit, heart, and mind, will then reveal to us the truth of God, the will of God. And in return, we will see ourselves overflowing even more in praying, worshiping, praising, and giving thanks to the Lord. It becomes like a wonderful heavenly circle.

chapter one
Prayer of Intercession

L ife becomes, day after day, so stressful and demanding that people must give the maximum of themselves to continue to perform and produce adequately. By this, we often don't have much time for others, nor much interest for our neighbours' situations.

Isn't the beauty of life found in sharing the suffering and tears of others?

> *Let each of you look out not only for his own interests, but also for the interests of others.*
>
> —Philippians 2:4

God is very pleased when we are concerned about other people's needs. Let us learn.

Pleading for Sodom

> *...but Abraham still stood before the Lord. And Abraham came near and said, "Would You also destroy the righteous with the wicked?"*
>
> —Genesis 18:22–23

Right after being informed by God about the gravity of the sin of Sodom and Gomorrah, and about the risk of God's imminent judgment against them, Abraham engaged in a vital intercession on behalf of the inhabitants of those two sister cities. It was as though he already felt the pain and suffering of the people there. Trusting in the Lord's righteousness and justice, he addressed to God, *"Would You also destroy the righteous with the wicked?"* (Genesis 18:23)

Amazingly, Abraham didn't put his own personal interest in first place. It would have been simple for him to ask favour from God for his nephew Lot, who lived there, and to let the others perish. In fact, the people of those two cities worked evil indeed, for God Himself said this about them: *"their sin was very grave"* (Genesis 18:20). But Abraham forgot himself and advocated for the children, youth, adults, elders, and families he didn't even know, fighting for their lives, pleading before God that their destruction might be avoided.

A MERCIFUL AND RIGHTEOUS GOD

First of all, note that Abraham started by acknowledging God for who He is: a compassionate, merciful, just, loving, kind God who would never punish the innocent instead of the guilty. Neither would He condemn the righteous with the wicked. Confident in the Lord's goodness, Abraham, with a heart full of love, sustained his plea. If there were just fifty righteous among the inhabitants of those cities—then just ten—would God show mercy and not destroy Sodom and Gomorrah? (Genesis 18:16–33) God showed Himself to be admirably patient in waiting for Abraham to reach the end of his intercession.

Genesis 18:27–28 expresses the profound respect and high reverence Abraham showed toward God:

Then Abraham answered and said, "Indeed now, I who am but dust and ashes have taken it upon myself to speak to the Lord: suppose there were five less than the fifty righteous; would You destroy all of the city for lack of five?"

So [the Lord] said, "If I find there forty-five, I will not destroy it."

Abraham and the Lord went on through their friendly, hearty dialogue until Abraham says to God,

"Let not the Lord be angry, and I will speak but once more: Suppose ten should be found there?"

And He said, "I will not destroy it for the sake of ten."

So the Lord went His way as soon as He had finished speaking with Abraham; and Abraham returned to his place.

—Genesis 18:32–33

PLEAD ON THEIR BEHALF

It is so touching to see that while almost all the people of Sodom and Gomorrah continued their lives as they pleased, driving themselves to destruction uncaringly and not even thinking about God, somebody far away who hadn't been their friend was pleading on their behalf. And they didn't know anything about it. I think there's enough here to bring us to realize how important it is to intercede for others under the eyes of the Lord, and also understand what God expects from us in prayer regarding our neighbours who are experiencing trials. When we say neighbours, we mean it according to the way the Bible sees it, and not only the people who live in the house next to ours.

Have you ever remembered someone in prayer, pleading before the Lord for their favour? Have you ever prayed on behalf of someone you don't even know? Someone somewhere may be in real need right now—in a hospital suffering lamentably, or in the loneliness of a desperate room with a bottle of alcohol his or her only faithful companion. This person may be asking him or herself, *What is the reason for me to continue to live?* It could also be someone in great need of prayer who's been involved in a car accident at this exact moment, or someone who's undergoing surgery in a hospital operating room. It could also be children or youth who have no parents, abandoned as easy prey to be devoured by the enemy of our soul, with no one who knows Jesus in their environment to stand on guard for them.

Let us pray for these people. Let us weep sincerely on their behalf. Let us intercede for their cause so that the mercy of God will reach them. That would be greatly pleasing to the Lord.

Daniel, for the Jews in Captivity

O Lord, according to all Your righteousness, I pray, let Your anger and Your fury be turned away from Your city Jerusalem, Your holy mountain; because for our sins, and for the iniquities of our fathers...

—Daniel 9:16

Such was the case of the prophet Daniel when he engaged himself in a prayer of favour for the people of Israel. According to Daniel 9:2–23, he was in Babylonian captivity for years and years. The Bible says that during this specific time, he came to understand by his readings that the desolation of Jerusalem and the Israelites' exile would be accomplished in seventy years, specified by the word of the Lord through Jeremiah the prophet. He therefore put himself in a position of prayer; he pleaded on behalf of his people in exile and the sanctuary of the Lord in their devastated homeland.

4

Then I set my face toward the Lord God to make request by prayer and supplications, with fasting, sackcloth, and ashes. And I prayed to the Lord my God, and made confession...
—Daniel 9:3–4

Again we must understand that the beginning of intercession requires that we clearly acknowledge God's righteousness, goodness, mercy, and faithfulness, and recognize at the same time how much we offend Him by transgressing His Word, His commandments.

O Lord, great and awesome God, who keeps His covenant and mercy with those who love Him, and with those who keep His commandments, we have sinned and committed iniquity, we have done wickedly and rebelled, even by departing from Your precepts and Your judgments.
—Daniel 9:4–5

Daniel, through his plea, carried and shared all the shame and blame that had fallen on the nation as a whole. Throughout his prayer, the prophet always said that "we" had sinned, not just "the people." He did not regard the fact that God considered him as His beloved. Not only did he associate himself with the disaster and disgrace of the people, but with tears he kept pleading on their behalf as though he himself had been the one to disobey.

...as it is this day—we have sinned, we have done wickedly!
—Daniel 9:15

The prophet Daniel never forgot that all glory belongs to the Lord. He recognized that nothing they had done could be considered good deeds, and they had no reason for God to answer their prayer; it could be done only because of God's great mercy and favour, His greatness and love for the place He had chosen to honour His name.

> *...for we do not present our supplications before You because of our righteous deeds, but because of Your great mercies. O Lord, hear! O Lord, forgive! O Lord, listen and act! Do not delay for Your own sake, my God, for Your city and Your people are called by Your name.*
>
> —Daniel 9:18–19

Finally, as we have seen, Daniel reminded God that it was for His great name that He would intervene in their favour. God will not suffer that His name be put to shame, because His name is great.

> *"For from the rising of the sun, even to its going down, My name shall be great among the Gentiles; in every place incense shall be offered to My name, and a pure offering; for My name shall be great among the nations," says the Lord of hosts.*
>
> —Malachi 1:11

And the Lord answered Daniel's prayer.

God sent an angel, Gabriel, to bring understanding to His servant Daniel about all things that would come relating to the future of the Jewish nation—from their time of captivity to the messianic age. Through a prophetic vision detailing seven weeks of time, as divinely interpreted by the angel of the Lord, the prophet received a clear explanation of the way this calamity of the Israeli people, and the shame upon the city and house of God in the motherland, would be brought to an end. It happened exactly the way the Lord God Almighty announced it through His angel to His servant.

...[Y]es, while I was speaking in prayer, the man Gabriel, whom I had seen in the vision at the beginning, being caused to fly swiftly, reached me about the time of the evening offering. And he informed me, and talked with me, and said, "O Daniel, I have now come forth to give you skill to understand. At the beginning of your supplications the command went out, and I have come to tell you, for you are greatly beloved; therefore consider the matter, and understand the vision: seventy weeks are determined for your people and for your holy city, to finish the transgression, to make an end of sins, to make reconciliation for iniquity, to bring in everlasting righteousness, to seal up vision and prophecy, and to anoint the Most Holy."

—Daniel 9:21–24

A BELOVED OF GOD

Here is another point we must not forget to underline: Daniel was a beloved of the Lord. The angel Gabriel said to Daniel, *"I have come to tell you, for you are greatly beloved"* (Daniel 9:23).

The highest mark of appreciation is when God approves someone, when He says about him or her, "I love the way you are. You please me so much." For such a person, it seems that almost all things are possible.

Here is what the Holy Spirit says in the Word of God:

When a man's ways please the Lord, he makes even his enemies to be at peace with him.

—Proverbs 16:7

Because he has set his love upon Me, therefore I will deliver him; I will set him on high, because he has known My name. He shall

7

call upon Me, and I will answer him; I will be with him in trouble; I will deliver him and honor him.

—Psalm 91:14–15

If God is for us, who can be against us?

—Romans 8:31

Everyone in need can address God for help, for answer and solutions, and the Lord will show mercy and compassion. But to those who faithfully obey Him and continue to walk in His way, not only will God intervene when they call but He will show to them His glory, for they are beloved.

So the Lord said to Moses, "I will also do this thing that you have spoken; for you have found grace in My sight, and I know you by name."
And he said, "Please, show me Your glory."

—Exodus 33:17–18

May you walk in the way of the Lord, and may He find great pleasure in you so that He allows you to experience His glory!

Apostle Paul, Voyage to Rome

...and indeed God has granted you all those who sail with you.
—Acts 27:24

I think it was the same spirit of caring for others, suffering with them, and being concerned about them in times of trouble that drove the apostle Paul, when divinely informed by the Holy Spirit that the voyage to Rome would end in disaster, with much loss not only of the cargo but also lives, to persuade them not to sail

(Acts 27:9). But the owner of the ship and the others didn't listen to him. The word of the apostle was fulfilled and they were beaten by terrible tempests on the sea for many days. They gave up all hope of being saved. They had food, but they abstained from eating, thus losing their appetites, because of fear and the gravity of the situation they were facing (Acts 27:33–34).

My God Has Given Your Lives to Me

But after the apostle Paul reproved them for not having listened to him before they left, he told them,

> *Men, you should have listened to me, and not have sailed from Crete and incurred this disaster and loss. And now I urge you to take heart, for there will be no loss of life among you, but only of the ship. For there stood by me this night an angel of the God to whom I belong and whom I serve, saying, "Do not be afraid, Paul; you must be brought before Caesar; and indeed God has granted you all those who sail with you." Therefore take heart, men, for I believe God that it will be just as it was told me.*
>
> —Acts 27:21–25

> *But the centurion... commanded that those who could swim should jump overboard first and get to land, and the rest, some on boards and some on parts of the ship. And so it was that they all escaped safely to land.*
>
> —Acts 27:43–44

Indeed, God had given all of their lives to the apostle, for there was no loss of human life. I believe that God saw the disposition of the apostle's heart, his constant prayer during their time of despair, the men's anxiety about the violence of the waves, their fear of imminent death, and the possible destruction of the ship. That's why He gave to Paul the lives of his companions.

Our God is indeed a faithful and merciful God who can surprise us for good when we pray and intercede for others with a pure and loving heart.

SOMEONE IS PRAYING FOR YOU

What a wonderful thing it is to know that someone somewhere is praying for you and me right now, carrying our burden to the Lord in our place, particularly in our moment of great need. It is good to realize that we aren't alone in the battle.

But it is indeed even more comforting to know that any condemnation against us will be reversed and will not prosper, for our Saviour Jesus Christ is seated at the right hand of the Father in heaven, and He intercedes for us, according to the book of Romans. So let us rejoice and be glad in the Lord.

> *Who is he who condemns? It is Christ who died, and furthermore is also risen, who is even at the right hand of God, who also makes intercession for us.*
>
> —Romans 8:34

Do you want to pray for someone else? Do you want to start now if you've not done so before? Do you want to think about someone in pain right now, someone suffering desperately without any hope, or someone alone after a tragic separation or the loss of a dear one? Would you like to tell God about it? What a great difference that would make!

Thank You, Lord Jesus!

chapter two

Prayer Seeking for God's Direction

Making a decision is one of the most familiar and important aspects of life that no one can avoid, except a baby. Whether you're young or elderly, we all make countless decisions every day, though some are of less importance and others of serious consequence.

The outcome of our decisions can give birth to unexpected situations, and those who have discernment never miss an opportunity to look for advice or wisdom before making a choice.

The Bible contains numerous accounts of significant people who regrettably, at certain moments of their lives, made poor decisions that led to destruction. Such was the case of Samson (Judges 14:1–3), who chose a Philistine woman as a wife. Because Philistines were among the enemies of Israel, he faced many challenges, obstacles, and situations he couldn't have survived by himself. And we know, sadly, how this ended (Judges 16:23–31).

We could very easily extend a long list of those who, for not enquiring the opinion of God first, put themselves and others around them in great trouble. Joshua, in the case of the Gibeonites, was one among many. Let us have a closer look!

Joshua Was Duped

We have come from a far country; now therefore, make a covenant with us.

—Joshua 9:6

The Bible tells us in Joshua 9:3–27 that the inhabitants of Gibeon heard about the way Joshua and the Israelites had treated Jericho and Ai, and how God, through them, destroyed great and renowned nations and kings on their way. So they were very afraid. They decided to disguise and present themselves to the Israeli people as ambassadors coming from a distant country, asking to make a covenant with them.

> *And they went to Joshua, to the camp at Gilgal, and said to him and to the men of Israel, "We have come from a far country; now therefore, make a covenant with us."*
>
> *Then the men of Israel said to the Hivites, "Perhaps you dwell among us; so how can we make a covenant with you?"*
>
> *But they said to Joshua, "We are your servants."*
>
> *And Joshua said to them, "Who are you, and where do you come from?"*
>
> *So they said to him: "From a very far country your servants have come, because of the name of the Lord your God; for we have heard of His fame, and all that He did in Egypt, and all that He did to the two kings of the Amorites who were beyond the Jordan—to Sihon king of Heshbon, and Og king of Bashan, who was at Ashtaroth. Therefore our elders and all the inhabitants of our country spoke to us, saying, 'Take provisions with you for*

the journey, and go to meet them, and say to them, "We are your servants; now therefore, make a covenant with us.""

—Joshua 9:6–11

It seems we aren't always as careful as we think we are.

Joshua and the Israelites counted a lot of victories on their journey, because they trusted in God and depended on Him for almost all their decisions. But they didn't remember to ask God for His opinion about them entering into covenant with these strangers.

The Bible says that Joshua and the leaders of Israel made a covenant of peace with the Gibeonites without consulting God. Right after, they discovered that those strangers had lied to them. This could all have been avoided if they had sought God's counsel first. Now, however, they didn't have any other choice but to respect their vow and let the Gibeonites live in their midst, against the command and will of the Lord. Because of that, the Israeli assembly was very upset.

Then the men of Israel took some of their provisions; but they did not ask counsel of the Lord. So Joshua made peace with them, and made a covenant with them to let them live; and the rulers of the congregation swore to them.

And it happened at the end of three days, after they had made a covenant with them, that they heard that they were their neighbors who dwelt near them...

Then Joshua called for them, and he spoke to them, saying, "Why have you deceived us, saying, 'We are very far from you,' when you dwell near us?..."

So they answered Joshua and said, "Because your servants were clearly told that the Lord your God commanded His servant Moses to give you all the land, and to destroy all the inhabitants of the land from before you; therefore we were very much afraid for our lives because of you, and have done this thing."

—Joshua 9:14–16, 22, 24

What a regrettable situation the people of Israel found themselves in. Unfortunately, they couldn't correct it. That's why we must always remember to go to God first and hear His thoughts about anything we decide to do.

Nevertheless, we have a number of people in the Bible who distinguished themselves through their good examples and total dependence on God. They wouldn't go anywhere or do anything without being assured that their actions were in accord with the will of God. Whatever decision they had to make, they asked and waited for God's opinion and approval. It's no surprise that they succeeded in all that they did.

Among them, we could easily mention King David, whose dedicated life to the Lord God remains a source of edification and inspiration for all.

David Escaped Danger of Death

Then David said, "Will the men of Keilah deliver me and my men into the hand of Saul?"

And the Lord said, "They will deliver you."

—1 Samuel 23:12

David developed a profound intimate relationship with God from a tender age. According to his own testimony to King Saul, he was still young when he started depending on the Lord for protection. In fact, his life had been put in danger many times as he shepherded the sheep of his father; he and his flock used to be attacked by wild and dangerous animals. But he overcame each time because God was always so close to him (1 Samuel 17:31–37).

That's why it's no surprise to see how important it was for David to inquire God's opinion after he discovered that King Saul had learned his location. The king had been possessed by an evil spirit and desired to kill David by any means.

> *Then David said, "O Lord God of Israel, Your servant has certainly heard that Saul seeks to come to Keilah to destroy the city for my sake. Will the men of Keilah deliver me into his hand? Will Saul come down, as Your servant has heard? O Lord God of Israel, I pray, tell Your servant."*
>
> *And the Lord said, "He will come down."*
>
> *Then David said, "Will the men of Keilah deliver me and my men into the hand of Saul?"*
>
> *And the Lord said, "They will deliver you."*
>
> *So David and his men, about six hundred, arose and departed from Keilah and went wherever they could go. Then it was told Saul that David had escaped from Keilah; so he halted the expedition.*
>
> —1 Samuel 23:10–13

God didn't let the people deliver His servant David to King Saul to be killed, for David sought the face of the Lord and obtained from Him instructions about what would happen if he remained. Then he left right away.

It is profitable to fearfully walk with the Lord, for He will never refuse to open Himself to His beloved. In times of need, He will send revelations necessary to guide us during our own journeys.

The secret of the Lord is with those who fear Him, and He will show them His covenant.

—Psalm 25:14

In any circumstance or situation, let us always go to the Lord through prayer and confidently expose all to Him. He will show to us the right direction to take. God has expressly said, *"I will instruct you and teach you in the way you should go; I will guide you with My eye"* (Psalm 32:8).

Why not invite Him right now, as you are reading, and submit everything to Him? He will give you divine instructions about the right decision to take for the situation you're facing this very moment. He will show you the way. Just trust Him.

We thank You, Lord!

David's Important Choice

It happened after this that David inquired of the Lord, saying, "Shall I go up to any of the cities of Judah?"
And the Lord said to him, "Go up."
David said, "Where shall I go up?"
And He said, "To Hebron."

—2 Samuel 2:1

Once again, we must appreciate the trust David put in the Lord. Being inspired from that, we should seriously consider involving God in everything we are doing today. So many mistakes, so much regret, so many tears, and so many failures could be avoided. Alas, God is very often the last One to be invited into our decision-making process—when He's not totally forgotten!

The Bible says after the death of King Saul, David, who had been anointed years prior by the prophet Samuel to become king over Israel, according to the will of God, decided to seek the face of the Lord to know what to do. That was very wise. What he had been waiting for a very long time had come, and he didn't want to miss the opportunity of a lifetime. Sometimes when we've been waiting for something important for a long time, excitement takes over and we lose our self-control. Not being able to think rightly, we mess everything up by making the wrong decisions.

David decided to avoid that at all costs.

> *...David inquired of the Lord, saying, "Shall I go up to any of the cities of Judah?"*
>> *And the Lord said to him, "Go up."*
>> *David said, "Where shall I go up?"*
>> *And He said, "To Hebron."*
>> *So David went up there...*
>> *Then the men of Judah came, and there they anointed David king over the house of Judah.*
>
> —2 Samuel 2:1–4

The Bible declares that after reigning seven years over Judah, David was crowned as king over the united nation of Israel. He became the greatest and most respected king the Israelites ever knew. Therefore, we often read God saying to the kings of Israel, "You have not been like my servant David."

> *...and tore the kingdom away from the house of David, and gave it to you; and yet you have not been as My servant David, who kept My commandments and who followed Me with all his heart, to do only what was right in My eyes.*
>
> —1 Kings 14:8

David became the standard that God used to measure all the other kings' godly character, whether in Judah or Israel. This was possible because God always came first in David's life.

Then all the tribes of Israel came to David at Hebron and spoke, saying, "Indeed we are your bone and your flesh. Also, in time past, when Saul was king over us, you were the one who led Israel out and brought them in; and the Lord said to you, 'You shall shepherd My people Israel, and be ruler over Israel.'"

Therefore all the elders of Israel came to the king at Hebron, and King David made a covenant with them at Hebron before the Lord. And they anointed David king over Israel. David was thirty years old when he began to reign, and he reigned forty years. In Hebron he reigned over Judah seven years and six months, and in Jerusalem he reigned thirty-three years over all Israel and Judah.

—2 Samuel 5:1–5

Because God controls time and circumstances, He chose for David to begin his reign in Hebron, even though He knew from the beginning that David would rule over all of Israel afterward. Hebron may have been the better soil for David to grow without great difficulties, so that he could be mature enough to later govern the Israeli nation as a whole with warm welcome from every part of the land. I'm sure that if he didn't inquire from the Lord first, he would have missed the opportunity to learn important strategies. Once again, let us thank God for always being available for us.

Lord, I thank You!

New Challenge, God's Strategy

*Then the Philistines went up once again and deployed themselves
in the Valley of Rephaim. Therefore David inquired of the Lord,
and He said, "You shall not go up..."*

—2 Samuel 5:22–23

The Bible informs us that the Philistines were in a rage when they
learned that David became king of the entire nation of Israel.
For sure they hadn't forgotten the lesson the God of Israel had
taught them through David when he had killed their hero, the
giant Goliath.

Without wasting any time, they deployed their army into po-
sitions of war against the children of Israel. And David, as usual,
sought for God's advice with the exactitude of his heart, without
neglecting any details:

*So David inquired of the Lord, saying, "Shall I go up against
the Philistines? Will You deliver them into my hand?"*

*And the Lord said to David, "Go up, for I will doubtless
deliver the Philistines into your hand."*

*So David went to Baal Perazim, and David defeated them
there; and he said, "The Lord has broken through my enemies
before me, like a breakthrough of water."*

—2 Samuel 5:19–20

I hope you understand the reality of the matter: the more
critical the situation is, the greater our dependence on the Lord
must be. That's why David took the time to explicitly ask God,
"Shall I go up?" and "Will You deliver them?"

We have seen that God patiently took the time to answer David according to each detail of his questions. This is reminiscent of God's conversation with Abraham when he pleaded on behalf of Sodom and Gomorrah (Genesis 18). God is so patient and kind; who could imagine that? God is always waiting for us to ask, and He is so gentle to take the time to answer. It is wonderful!

DAVID INQUIRED AGAIN

The Bible states in 2 Samuel 5:22 that the Philistines went up once again to attack Israel.

In moments like this, we could easily be tempted to conclude that because it's the same war, the same enemy, and about the same time, it wouldn't be necessary to ask God once again for His opinion. Many of us have failed in similar situations, but thank God that David wouldn't take that chance. He understood that whether or not God had already given prior instructions, he had to make sure the Lord was with him, beside him, and that they were both in agreement. If he didn't have God's approbation on any matter, he wouldn't make that decision. Oh how important it is for us today as well to act like David.

We read that David once again spoke to God before engaging this new deployment of combat. Like before, he asked God if he should go up; surprisingly, this time things were different. The Lord's answer was he shouldn't go up, for some new strategies needed to take place.

We fail to depend entirely on God at our own risk, for everything in this world is dominated by evil, where the power to kill, to steal, and to destroy is more than imminent. The devil is constantly looking by all kinds of evil means to deceive us, mislead us, disappoint us, waste our lives, and if possible bring us to nothing, reduce us to complete failure, and take our lives. But praise God, we have a friend in Jesus; we have a Father who is our

God. And we know that greater is He who is in us than he who is in the world (1 John 4:4).

> *Be sober, be vigilant; because your adversary the devil walks about like a roaring lion, seeking whom he may devour.*
>
> —1 Peter 5:8

Amazingly, by his faithful dependence on the Lord, David overcame his enemies, the Philistines. God Himself intervened in the battle, so David was not put to shame. The Bible says that the enemy was greatly defeated.

> *Then the Philistines went up once again and deployed themselves in the Valley of Rephaim. Therefore David inquired of the Lord, and He said, "You shall not go up; circle around behind them, and come upon them in front of the mulberry trees. And it shall be, when you hear the sound of marching in the tops of the mulberry trees, then you shall advance quickly. For then the Lord will go out before you to strike the camp of the Philistines." And David did so, as the Lord commanded him; and he drove back the Philistines from Geba as far as Gezer.*
>
> —2 Samuel 5:22–25

The only thing we can say after that is, "This is wonderful!"

Do as the Lord Commands

However, there is one point we should not forget: "*And David did so, as the Lord commanded him*" (2 Samuel 5:25).

It's one thing to ask for God's advice before acting; it's another thing to commit oneself to obey Him. Sometimes we face danger and we inquire from God. It is then easy to do what God says, because it will be for our rescue and safety. But when the

Word of God requires our faith and submission, because we don't yet see or understand exactly where the instruction of God will lead us, will we accept what He says? Perhaps we expected to hear the opposite Word from the Lord instead of what He says to us. Will we obey and go according to the suggestion of the Lord? Yes, we must do it in complete accord with God's opinion. We must obey God's decision, which is the best. It is a great privilege to know God's mind about anything that's still to come; in this way, we will never be mistaken. This is a demonstration of God's love for His people. Lord, we adore You! Thank You, Jesus.

Then Manoah Prayed

O my Lord, please let the Man of God whom You sent come to us again and teach us what we shall do...

—Judges 13:8

Let us conclude this section with the experience of a man named Manoah, whose wife was barren, so they had no children.

The Bible tells us in Judges 13:1–13 that the Israelites had once again been delivered by God to be oppressed by their enemies because they had done evil in the face of the Lord. Forty years later, God decided to intervene for their rescue. He sent His angel to Manoah's wife, announcing to her that she would conceive a male child who would deliver Israel out of the hand of the Philistines. And she received from the angel very special advice concerning the child, because he would be dedicated to God all his life.

And He said to me, "Behold, you shall conceive and bear a son. Now drink no wine or similar drink, nor eat anything unclean, for the child shall be a Nazirite to God from the womb to the day of his death."

—Judges 13:7

A RESPONSIBLE PARENT

Manoah was absent at the coming of the angel. As soon as he returned, being informed about the announcement, he put himself right away into prayer so that God could reveal to him exact instructions about the child and what they should do as parents.

Then Manoah prayed to the Lord, and said, "O my Lord, please let the Man of God whom You sent come to us again and teach us what we shall do for the child who will be born."

—Judges 13:8

The Bible says that God answered the prayer of Manoah and sent the angel to the family a second time, for God listens to prayers. We have to appreciate Manoah's sense of responsibility, for he could have easily accepted his wife's information and been satisfied; in fact, the news that they would soon have a child could have been more than enough. But considering the particularity of that child in the sight of God and the importance of his mission in the midst of the children of Israel, Manoah decided to inquire from the Lord how to care for the child according to God's will and learn their responsibilities toward that child.

Then the woman ran in haste and told her husband, and said to him, "Look, the Man who came to me the other day has just now appeared to me!"

So Manoah arose and followed his wife. When he came to the Man, he said to Him, "Are You the Man who spoke to this woman?"

And He said, "I am."

Manoah said, "Now let Your words come to pass! What will be the boy's rule of life, and his work?"

So the Angel of the Lord said to Manoah, "Of all that I said to the woman let her be careful. She may not eat anything that comes from the vine, nor may she drink wine or similar drink, nor eat anything unclean. All that I commanded her let her observe."

—Judges 13:10–14

I like the words of the King James Version version for Manoah's request to the angel: *"How shall we order the child, and how shall we do unto him?"* (Judges 13:12, KJV)

GOD IS CONCERNED ABOUT THE CHILD IN THE WOMB

Manoah took this matter very seriously, and we should learn an important lesson from it. When children are on their way to us, are we concerned enough about God's plan for them that we pray and inquire from God about their lives, their future, their destiny, and the kind of godly care we should give them, even while they are still in the womb? Do we sincerely ask God to reveal His opinion, His will about our children before they have been born? Let us confess the truth: if we did so, and God answered us, we would learn the best way to wait for our child. Look at what God said about Jeremiah the prophet:

Before I formed you in the womb I knew you; before you were born I sanctified you; I ordained you a prophet to the nations.

—Jeremiah 1:5

I am reminded of a well-known evangelist minister who during a service prophesied to a woman that God was about to give her a male child, and that the child would become a prophet. Because the woman didn't want any more children, she protested vigorously against the Word of the servant of God. Unexpectedly for her, after a while she became pregnant and gave birth to a male child; the boy grew up and afterwards became a prophet. Now that child is ministering under the office and gift of prophecy in many places, churches, and countries for the edification of the body of Christ and the glory of God.

We must be careful when we don't know something. We need wisdom to learn how to deal with what tomorrow will bring. It's good for us to plan, decide, and act throughout our lives—to create, to build, and to conquer. But we must remember to submit our actions to the Lord through prayer and seek His direction first.

In Proverbs, the Bible gives us profitable instructions and warnings that we shouldn't neglect:

> *Commit your works to the Lord, and your thoughts will be established... A man's heart plans his way, but the Lord directs his steps.*
>
> —Proverbs 16:3, 9

> *There are many plans in a man's heart, nevertheless the Lord's counsel—that will stand.*
>
> —Proverbs 19:21

May the Lord lead you and meet you at your moment of needs, as you choose to hear from Him first.

chapter three
Prayer with Unexpected Answers

Whenever we pray, we can always expect an answer, for it is a fact that God listens to prayer. Because of that, many will come to the Lord in prayer and wait for an answer from Him. The Bible confirms it: *"O You who hear prayer, to You all flesh will come"* (Psalm 65:2).

For us Christians, believers in God our Father through Christ Jesus our Saviour and Lord, it is normal to pray and see the intervention of God. But what needs to be underlined here is that sometimes, because of the nature of our needs or the reason we pray, we would like to dictate to God the type of answer He should give. We even estimate the time when we should receive it. We consider our situation to be an emergency, or the pain very hard, which could be true. However, we easily forget that God knows better than we do what is best for us.

The Bible tells the stories of people in the past who prayed and hoped confidently to have an answer from God which would bring them satisfaction and solutions to their problems. But they sometimes, surprisingly, received quite the opposite of what they expected. Among them, a very few have been selected for the purpose of this book. Let us be inspired as we learn from their experiences.

God Knows Better

Concerning this thing I pleaded with the Lord three times that it might depart from me. And He said to me, "My grace is sufficient for you..."

—2 Corinthians 12:8

1 Corinthians 13:9 makes it clear that as humans *"we know in part."* We cannot have the whole picture. Only God knows everything and the reasons behind everything. That's why the Lord says that His ways are not our ways. What we can see and understand is subject to our human capacity to see and comprehend, but God is limitless in His wisdom and might. We can see only what we as humans can handle, but God has it all as a whole.

In 2 Corinthians 12:1–10, the apostle Paul speaks with humility about a person (in fact, himself) who had the grace and divine favour to visit the third heaven and Paradise. The Bible adds that he even heard inexpressible words, which is not lawful for a man to utter. Such a privilege could cause someone to boast, but God loves us so much that He wouldn't let any of us be lost. The way that the Lord works may not be satisfactory for us, because we may not often understand it, but He acts with our best interests at heart, for our eternal gain.

For what profit is it to a man if he gains the whole world, and loses his own soul? Or what will a man give in exchange for his soul?

—Matthew 16:26

The apostle details how he pleaded with the Lord to deliver him from an affliction in his life. He describes it as *"a messenger of Satan to buffet me"* (2 Corinthians 12:7). From this, we understand that it was something very painful, and he would do his best to be separated from it. That's why he insisted before the Lord in prayer for an answer:

> *And lest I should be exalted above measure by the abundance of the revelations, a thorn in the flesh was given to me, a messenger of Satan to buffet me, lest I be exalted above measure. Concerning this thing I pleaded with the Lord three times that it might depart from me. And He said to me, "My grace is sufficient for you, for My strength is made perfect in weakness." Therefore most gladly I will rather boast in my infirmities, that the power of Christ may rest upon me.*
>
> —2 Corinthians 12:7–9

At first Paul wanted to be set free from this calamity at all costs. As a human who was suffering, it was normal for him to look to the Lord for relief. But as one who had given all to the Lord, conscious of the price of the heavenly call and the reward attached to it, it's obvious that the pain and suffering finally became secondary. Paul came to see his affliction as an opportunity to stay close to God:

> *For I consider that the sufferings of this present time are not worthy to be compared with the glory which shall be revealed in us.*
>
> —Romans 8:18

In the end, we have no choice but to cooperate with God, even though we don't understand, because His thoughts are above ours. Read what He says in the book of Isaiah:

> *"For My thoughts are not your thoughts, nor are your ways My ways," says the Lord. "For as the heavens are higher than the*

earth, so are My ways higher than your ways, and My thoughts than your thoughts."

—Isaiah 55:8–9

All of this makes me think of the story of Job. Job couldn't understand why that terrible affliction fell upon him and his family, so he probably asked himself many questions which went unanswered. His prayer also seemed to go unheard. In that circumstance, any of us would wonder, *Where is God while I suffer greatly?*

Why did I not die at birth? Why did I not perish when I came from the womb? Why did the knees receive me? Or why the breasts, that I should nurse? For now I would have lain still and been quiet, I would have been asleep; then I would have been at rest...

—Job 3:11–13

But in the end, when the Lord decided to reveal His majesty, omnipotence, and sovereignty, Job couldn't help but bow down, repent, and ask for forgiveness. He had no choice but to accept the fact that God indeed has the last Word and the last decision. Let us hear a few words of God's intervention:

Who is this who darkens counsel by words without knowledge? Now prepare yourself like a man; I will question you, and you shall answer Me.
Where were you when I laid the foundations of the earth? Tell Me, if you have understanding.

—Job 38:2–4

The Lord continued to interrogate Job, but in the end Job realized that not only did he have no argument but God's reason can be totally above our understanding and comprehension. We have to remember that God will always decide for our good, and His name will always be glorified. Truly, He is worthy to be praised.

You asked, "Who is this who hides counsel without knowledge?" Therefore I have uttered what I did not understand, things too wonderful for me, which I did not know... I have heard of You by the hearing of the ear, but now my eye sees You. Therefore I abhor myself, and repent in dust and ashes.

—Job 42:3, 5–6

The Bible says that because Job stayed faithful to God in his time of trials, even though his prayer didn't change his condition of affliction and suffering, God wasn't unresponsive to his pain. In His own time, God brought total restoration to Job's life, and gave him two times the blessings compared to all that he'd had before.

And the Lord restored Job's losses when he prayed for his friends... Now the Lord blessed the latter days of Job more than his beginning.

—Job 42:10, 12

GOD WANTS US TO FORGIVE

A last important point we will consider about Job's misadventure is this: God restored Job's losses after he prayed for his friends. Job didn't allow his affliction to prevent him from giving glory and honour to God. In fact, from the beginning his reaction, after he had lost all his property and children, was:

Naked I came from my mother's womb, and naked shall I return there. The Lord gave, and the Lord has taken away; blessed be

*the name of the Lord. In all this Job did not sin nor charge God
with wrong.*

—Job 1:21–22

Even after the devil attacked his personal health, and his
own wife suggested that he curse God, in the midst of this terrible disaster Job demonstrated that his integrity in the Lord
wasn't subject to happiness or good times. Therefore, he rebuked
his wife strongly.

*Then his wife said to him, "Do you still hold fast to your integri-
ty? Curse God and die!"*

*But he said to her, "You speak as one of the foolish women
speaks. Shall we indeed accept good from God, and shall we not
accept adversity?" In all this Job did not sin with his lips.*

—Job 2:9–10

Even though someone may be nice, almost without reproach,
as soon as trials and suffering come knocking at his door, people
start to judge; they give interpretations one way or another, gos-
siping about what has happened to him. Even those who were
close friends before become quite distant.

The three friends of Job offended him severely throughout
his time of testing, condemning him as if he was a devoted crim-
inal, an unforgivable sinner, accusing him wrongly instead of reminding him of God's goodness, faithfulness, righteousness, and
compassion. They were not a source of comfort. The anger of
God was provoked against the three friends because of the way
they treated Job, and all because they couldn't understand the
way of God, the mind of God.

And so it was, after the Lord had spoken these words to Job, that the Lord said to Eliphaz the Temanite, "My wrath is aroused against you and your two friends, for you have not spoken of Me what is right, as My servant Job has. Now therefore, take for yourselves seven bulls and seven rams, go to My servant Job, and offer up for yourselves a burnt offering; and My servant Job shall pray for you. For I will accept him, lest I deal with you according to your folly; because you have not spoken of Me what is right, as My servant Job has."

—Job 42:7–8

God restored Job after he prayed for his friends, who had mistreated him as badly as he had suffered. Indeed, we can imagine that the prayer of Job for those friends wasn't to curse them but to ask forgiveness from God for them, to call favour and the blessing of God upon their lives. God made it clear: *"and My servant Job shall pray for you. For I will accept him, lest I deal with you according to your folly"* (Job 42:8). This reminds us that to ask God's forgiveness for people, we must have already forgiven them of all offences they may have caused us. Moreover, we must pray for them with the love of God and with a pure heart, a heart that can sincerely love them in a way that's pleasing to God, for God wants us to forgive.

And whenever you stand praying, if you have anything against anyone, forgive him, that your Father in heaven may also forgive you your trespasses.

—Mark 11:25

Since we always come to God in prayer, whether for ourselves or for others, we must be at peace with one another, and also with God. Thus, nothing will come to hinder our prayer.

Finally, the lesson from this is that we must trust God always, even though we don't understand. The answer to our prayer is not necessarily according to what we initially expected; later on, we will realize that the Lord has given us what we really needed, what is in His plan for our lives so that His greatness, power, and love may be demonstrated in and through us for His glory and in the name of His precious Son Jesus Christ.

When Faith Is Really Tested

Have mercy on me, O Lord, Son of David! My daughter is severely demon-possessed.

—Matthew 15:22

It is very comforting as Christians to know that we can call upon the name of Jesus in times of trouble and find deliverance in Him, and moreover a faithful friend at all times. That is our consolation. In fact, Jesus Himself says, *"Come to Me, all you who labor and are heavy laden, and I will give you rest"* (Matthew 11:28).

That's why great multitudes used to follow Jesus during the time of His ministry on earth. The Bible says that He was always moved with compassion for them. He went around healing their sick, setting their captives free from the oppression of the enemy, and speaking to them the Word of eternal salvation.

When evening had come, they brought to Him many who were demon-possessed. And He cast out the spirits with a word, and healed all who were sick...

—Matthew 8:16

And that very hour He cured many of infirmities, afflictions, and evil spirits; and to many blind He gave sight.

—Luke 7:21

And when Jesus went out He saw a great multitude; and He was moved with compassion for them, and healed their sick.

—Matthew 14:14

But when Jesus knew it, He withdrew from there. And great multitudes followed Him, and He healed them all.

—Matthew 12:15

Then great multitudes came to Him, having with them the lame, blind, mute, maimed, and many others; and they laid them down at Jesus' feet, and He healed them.

—Matthew 15:30

As we have seen so far, many of those who were in need, and could come close to Jesus, had the grace to obtain from Him healings, deliverance, and favour.

A FOREIGN WOMAN OF FAITH

This wasn't so easy for a certain woman, described in Matthew 15:21–28, whose faith was severely tested during her encounter with Jesus. Her experience serves as an example for all those who can admire the power of endurance, perseverance, patience, humility, and the fear of the Lord in the life of this great woman of faith.

In Matthew 15:21, Jesus withdrew Himself, as He typically did, and went to the area of Tyre and Sidon, which was not Jewish territory. There He met a Canaanite woman who cried out for favour from the Lord because her daughter was demon-possessed.

She was not Jewish and didn't belong to those who should have had the privilege of waiting for the promise of the coming Messiah—the Son of David, who according to prophecies of the Old Testament would come to bring deliverance and peace to Israel, the people of God.

Despite being an outcast, that woman found the way to know and believe that Jesus Christ was the Son of God, the One who was supposed to come, and the Son of David whom Israel was waiting for. With an open heart, she cried out, *"Have mercy on me, O Lord, Son of David! My daughter is severely demon-possessed"* (Matthew 15:22). We can easily imagine the great hope with which she put in this request, because she had surely heard that Jesus healed the sick and cast out demons.

The first surprise is that Jesus didn't answer her at all; the Son of God did not pay any attention to her. The Bible tells us that the disciples of Jesus pressed Him to send her away, for she didn't stop crying after the Lord for help. Jesus finally opened His mouth and reminded her harshly that He hadn't come for strangers, but to save those of the house of Israel.

Many of us today would be disappointed at this situation. We present our problem to the Lord, we pray, and not only does God ignore us but He multiplies His blessings and favours to others as if we didn't exist. But there was something inside that woman that was greater and stronger than the hindrance to her prayer. The refusal of the Master couldn't stop her from continuing to cry out to Him or going closer.

The Bible says that she moved forward to a higher level: she worshipped Him. With the eyes of our heart we can see this woman, a tearful mother who knows there is no other solution for her daughter's situation. There probably wouldn't be another opportunity like this again. She bowed down, and with a deep suffering voice she cried, *"Lord, help me!"* (Matthew 15:25)

But His answer was as discouraging as before, or even worse. This time, the Lord made it clear that she was an outcast and didn't deserve what she was begging for. He used an analogy about children's bread not being thrown to the dogs. Then, with a determination that nothing on earth could defeat, the Canaanite woman answered, *"Yes, Lord, but even the little dogs eat the crumbs which fall from their masters' table"* (Matthew 15:27).

At that moment, the woman showed that she understood that the hope of Israel and all humanity rested on the anointed Son of God, the Messiah. She also proved that she had the faith to attract the attention of God.

So her request reached the heart of Jesus, who exclaimed, *"O woman, great is your faith!"* (Matthew 15:28) The Bible adds that she obtained what she had prayed for.

The Bible says that without faith it is impossible to please God (Hebrews 11:6). The Canaanite woman demonstrated an example of the work of faith, an example that should inspire us. We must believe that our prayers are heard from heaven, even when God keeps silent and our circumstances seem to get more difficult. In such a case, only our faith will be able to sustain us and help us to keep going on.

Jesus adds, *"If you can believe, all things are possible to him who believes"* (Mark 9:23). The woman had been ignored, rebuked, scorned, and humiliated, but she didn't quit because she knew that Jesus was able and trustworthy. Therefore she believed in Him. With endurance, she continued to cry, to persist in her petition. Then she was recognized by the Saviour as a woman of great faith; her daughter was also delivered.

What a wonderful testimony! Let us stand strong in our faith, believing that God will always keep His promises.

chapter four
Prayer in the Midst of Affliction

As human beings, we receive from God the ability to produce, create, perform, build, and conquer, among many other things. Some of us have been granted notorious qualifications to achieve these things with great honour. Others, by their natural skills, work hard and make their names of notable renown.

But the reality remains: no human can preview the future with exactitude or have total control over circumstances yet to come. Just when we think ourselves to be the most secure, in a fraction of a second everything could change if not for God's intervention. That should be enough to make us aware of our insufficiency, and call us to trust in the Lord instead of our own possessions or achievements, even though they are valuable. Many tragedies around the world speak for themselves in this matter; the Bible records many stories of people whose lives turned to desolation at a time when they didn't expect it.

Trusting Under Trial

Thus says the Lord: "Set your house in order, for you shall die, and not live."

—2 Kings 20:1

We read in the Bible about King Hezekiah, who reigned over Judah for a period of twenty-nine years. He found himself right in the sight of the Lord, according to all that his father David had done (2 Chronicles 29:2). In fact, the Bible lets us know that King Hezekiah spent almost all the time of his reign working hard to bring the people of Israel back to the Lord, after all the immoralities and corruptions that Judah had been led to by his father, King Ahaz, whose heart hadn't been right with God. Ahaz had led the people of God to all the abominations of the nations whom the Lord had cast out before the children of Israel. Here's how the reality of Ahaz's behaviour was described:

He burned incense in the Valley of the Son of Hinnom, and burned his children in the fire, according to the abominations of the nations whom the Lord had cast out before the children of Israel. And he sacrificed and burned incense on the high places, on the hills, and under every green tree.

—2 Chronicles 28:3–4

Because of his evildoing, God delivered Judah into the hands of the enemies of Israel. The Syrians, Assyrians, Edomites, and Philistines multiplied their attacks against them. In spite of that, King Ahaz did not turn to the Lord.

Now in the time of his distress King Ahaz became increasingly unfaithful to the Lord. This is that King Ahaz... And in every single city of Judah he made high places to burn incense to other gods, and provoked to anger the Lord God of his fathers.

—2 Chronicles 28:22, 25

It was in this atmosphere that King Hezekiah inherited the throne. From the beginning of his reign, King Hezekiah had a sincere heart for the Lord; his desire was to bring back not only Judah but Israel as a whole to the Lord God. Without any wasting of time, he put himself to work, gathering the Levites and priests and commanding them to sanctify themselves. He charged them to clean and sanctify the house of the Lord.

Then, after the cleansing of the temple, King Hezekiah restored the temple worship, which had been interrupted for a long time. He appointed the musicians, the Levites and the priests with their instruments, and the singers with the songs of worship, according to the commandment of David.

Then he brought in the priests and the Levites, and gathered them in the East Square, and said to them: "Hear me, Levites! Now sanctify yourselves, sanctify the house of the Lord God of your fathers, and carry out the rubbish from the holy place. For our fathers have trespassed and done evil in the eyes of the Lord our God; they have forsaken Him, have turned their faces away from the dwelling place of the Lord, and turned their backs on Him.

—2 Chronicles 29:4–6

KING HEZEKIAH'S COMMITMENT

Now it is in my heart to make a covenant with the Lord God of Israel, that His fierce wrath may turn away from us. My sons, do not be negligent now, for the Lord has chosen you to stand before Him, to serve Him, and that you should minister to Him and burn incense...

Then Hezekiah commanded them to offer the burnt offering on the altar. And when the burnt offering began, the song of the Lord also began, with the trumpets and with the instruments of David king of Israel. So all the assembly worshiped, the singers sang, and the trumpeters sounded; all this continued until the

burnt offering was finished. And when they had finished offering,
the king and all who were present with him bowed and worshiped.

—2 Chronicles 29:10–11, 27–29

Like an evangelist, King Hezekiah worked hard to involve the entire nation of Israel in the move of revival he had initiated. He sent letters of invitation to all of Judah and Israel to come to the house of the Lord at Jerusalem and keep the Passover of the Lord God of Israel (2 Chronicles 30:1). He gave himself totally to the cause of the Lord his God, the God of Israel.

Then the runners went throughout all Israel and Judah with the
letters from the king and his leaders, and spoke according to the
command of the king: "Children of Israel, return to the Lord God
of Abraham... Now do not be stiff-necked, as your fathers were,
but yield yourselves to the Lord; and enter His sanctuary, which
He has sanctified forever, and serve the Lord your God, that the
fierceness of His wrath may turn away from you... for the Lord
your God is gracious and merciful, and will not turn His face from
you if you return to Him.

—2 Chronicles 30:6, 8–9

The zeal of the King for the work of the Lord and his perseverance produced fruit. In fact, the Bible says that multitudes from everywhere came to Jerusalem to worship in the temple of the Lord God of Israel (2 Chronicles 30:18–20). In spite of intimidation, pressure, and mockery, which he received many times from the enemies of Israel, his heart stood steadfast in trusting the Lord.

HEZEKIAH'S UNEXPECTED NEWS

But the Bible declares in 2 Kings 20:1 that in those days Hezekiah was sick. God sent the prophet Isaiah to inform him that he must put his house in order, for he was going to die. I think King Hezekiah was shocked when the message came to him. It's part of the reality of life that we eventually become sick, though it's not currently a normal and acceptable situation. But at least while we're sick, we can maintain hope that we will eventually be healed. I imagine that it was so for the King, who had been an obedient servant of the Lord, loving his God, serving Him faithfully, and being loyal to Him with all his heart without any reproach.

It is obvious that during his affliction, King Hezekiah kept praying and expected that one day God was going to heal him, particularly since he was only thirty-nine years old. But with that terrible news from the prophet Isaiah, like any human being, the king started to review his life, realizing that his days had been short. He didn't even have time to enjoy life as a king.

Where else could he go for help? God had always been his refuge in times of trouble, and the prophet had regularly been the mediator through whom Hezekiah received from God. But unfortunately, in this crucial moment of affliction, the Word of God from the prophet that should have brought hope to him was anything but hopeful: *"Thus says the Lord: 'Set your house in order, for you shall die, and not live'"* (2 Kings 20:1).

In other words, "You are going to die."

That's why the Bible says he wept bitterly as he turned his face toward the wall and prayed, *"Where can I go from Your Spirit? Or where can I flee from Your presence?"* (Psalm 139:7)

Where can we go from the Presence of the Lord? The answer is nowhere. We need God, and we will always need Him. As Jesus says in John 15:5, *"for without Me you can do nothing."*

Understand that King Hezekiah was deeply sad not only because he was suffering but because he was conscious of his inability to help himself. He already knew the position of God in the matter, which meant that almost all was done for him, and he couldn't expect to have any more hope for his healing.

When we take a closer look at the situation, we can say that he wasn't ready for the last evolution of his condition; he hadn't expected his end on earth to come this way, or so quickly. Let us see what the Bible says next:

Then he turned his face toward the wall, and prayed to the Lord, saying, "Remember now, O Lord, I pray, how I have walked before You in truth and with a loyal heart, and have done what was good in Your sight." And Hezekiah wept bitterly.

And it happened, before Isaiah had gone out into the middle court, that the word of the Lord came to him, saying, "Return and tell Hezekiah the leader of My people, 'Thus says the Lord, the God of David your father: "I have heard your prayer, I have seen your tears; surely I will heal you. On the third day you shall go up to the house of the Lord. And I will add to your days fifteen years..."'"

—2 Kings 20:2–6

King Hezekiah was in a position to lose hope, but in the hopelessness of his cause he grabbed the only means of rescue he had access to: he decided to go to God in prayer anyway. As believers in God, it is our privilege, our security, to go to our Lord in times of distress, even though we don't feel His presence or doubt that we deserve His attention. The Bible says, *"Call upon Me in the day of trouble; I will deliver you, and you shall glorify Me"* (Psalm 50:15).

But as for Hezekiah, God's pronouncement had already been made. He would die. His case to survive on earth had become hopeless. Reversing this was impossible and out of his hands. Maybe, in that moment, he remembered how Moses, in a similar situation, had begged God to let him enter the Promised Land, a request which had been refused (Deuteronomy 3:23–26).

HEZEKIAH'S PRAYER

Conscious of the critical nature of his situation, King Hezekiah offered to God a prayer quite special; he went to the heart of God. He went where all his treasures had been stored, where all his efforts and energies had been spent:

> *Remember now, O Lord, I pray, how I have walked before You in truth and with a loyal heart, and have done what was good in Your sight.*
>
> —2 Kings 20:3

Through this prayer, we can feel the pain and agony of the king's soul, but at the same time we cannot set aside the humility and respect of a loyal servant for his Lord. Like a child who powerlessly grabs the legs or hands of his parents as he is being chastised by them, he doesn't even ask for healing. Instead he submits himself with reverence to the mercy of the only God he had, his only Help. Opening his pure heart without any reproach toward Him, his face turned toward the wall, and weeping bitterly, King Hezekiah offered this simple and deep prayer, the expression of a trusting heart under trial.

Such a cry from the deep heart of a faithful servant couldn't easily escape the attention of the Lord. God listens to prayers and answers them as He decides—and this is for our good. But we cannot underestimate the fact that there is a connection, something meaningful, between prayer from an upright heart and the orientation of God's answer, for God is always interested to the state of our heart. Matthew 5:8 says, *"Blessed are the pure in heart, for they shall see God."*

When we read about Zacharias and his wife Elizabeth, the parents of John the Baptist, we find that they couldn't have a child, and they were well advanced in years. Here's what the Bible says about them:

And they were both righteous before God, walking in all the commandments and ordinances of the Lord blameless.

—Luke 1:6

They continued to serve the Lord faithfully. One day, during the exercise of his duty for the Lord, Zacharias had an encounter with an angel from God—and their needs from that moment were met. The prayer they had prayed for a long time had been answered, for God gave him and his wife a child.

But the angel said to him, "Do not be afraid, Zacharias, for your prayer is heard; and your wife Elizabeth will bear you a son, and you shall call his name John."

—Luke 1:13

GOD'S ANSWER TO HEZEKIAH

The Bible says that the Lord heard the king's prayer. He had seen the tears of His servant, and He healed him.

And it happened, before Isaiah had gone out into the middle court, that the word of the Lord came to him, saying, "Return and tell Hezekiah the leader of My people, 'Thus says the Lord, the God of David your father: "I have heard your prayer, I have seen your tears; surely I will heal you."'"

—2 Kings 20:4–5

There is enough here for us to be encouraged and inspired when life suddenly puts us in a situation to seek the face of the Lord, who can see the tears of His people. King Hezekiah gave his entire life to pleasing God. I don't think he had in mind that those efforts for God's sake would be counted one day, seeing that God would have to hear a last request with tears from him, but the result was that God did consider them.

Since we don't know about tomorrow, let us take account of these words of Jesus, and gain wisdom:

Do not lay up for yourselves treasures on earth, where moth and rust destroy and where thieves break in and steal; but lay up for yourselves treasures in heaven, where neither moth nor rust destroys and where thieves do not break in and steal. For where your treasure is, there your heart will be also.

—Matthew 6:19–21

Finally, keep in mind that God will always remember your efforts for His cause, and when we least expect Him, He will show Himself. The question we must ask ourselves now is this: will the treasures we have stored so far with great effort be counted by God one day, whether here on earth or above? Think about it seriously.

For God is not unjust to forget your work and labor of love which you have shown toward His name, in that you have ministered to the saints, and do minister.

—Hebrews 6:10

Remember that God always listens to prayer.

In Bitterness of Soul

O Lord of hosts, if You will indeed look on the affliction of Your maidservant and remember me, and not forget Your maidservant, but will give Your maidservant a male child, then I will give...

—1 Samuel 1:11

Suffering in the company of people who cannot understand your pain can sometimes have a greater effect than the affliction itself. We tend to expect to receive comfort, support, and encouragement from our friends and family in moments of distress. This is normal.

Such was the case of Hannah, whose husband Elkanah had two wives. One was Peninnah, who gave birth to many children, and the other was Hannah, whose womb God had closed so she couldn't have any child (1 Samuel 1:1–2). Hannah had to bear the daily pain of not being able to conceive. As if this wasn't enough, she was continually provoked by her rival, Peninnah, because of her barren condition. Her life was sorrowful, miserable, and full of tears. Her husband, who loved her even more than Peninnah, couldn't understand the depth of Hannah's suffering either.

Then Elkanah her husband said to her, "Hannah, why do you weep? Why do you not eat? And why is your heart grieved? Am I not better to you than ten sons?"

—1 Samuel 1:8

This scene of atrocity repeated itself every year when Elkanah took the family up from their city to worship and sacrifice to the Lord in Shiloh, where Eli and his two sons ministered as the priests (1 Samuel 1:3). The Bible continues to describe the bitterness of Hannah's soul:

And her rival also provoked her severely, to make her miserable, because the Lord had closed her womb. So it was, year by year, when she went up to the house of the Lord, that she provoked her; therefore she wept and did not eat.

—1 Samuel 1:6–7

HANNAH SEEKS GOD'S HELP

Hannah decided to seek help from the Lord. She prayed and asked God to give her a male child, and she promised to consecrate him to the service of the Lord.

And she was in bitterness of soul, and prayed to the Lord and wept in anguish. Then she made a vow and said, "O Lord of hosts, if You will indeed look on the affliction of Your maidservant and remember me, and not forget Your maidservant, but will give Your maidservant a male child, then I will give him to the Lord all the days of his life, and no razor shall come upon his head."

—1 Samuel 1:10–11

The Bible says that she was so deep in prayer, as she poured out her suffering before the Lord, that even the priest Eli had been mistaken on her appearance, presuming that she was drunk.

And it happened, as she continued praying before the Lord, that Eli watched her mouth. Now Hannah spoke in her heart; only her lips moved, but her voice was not heard. Therefore Eli thought she was drunk. So Eli said to her, "How long will you be drunk? Put your wine away from you!"

But Hannah answered and said, "No, my lord, I am a woman of sorrowful spirit. I have drunk neither wine nor intoxicating drink, but have poured out my soul before the Lord. "Do not consider your maidservant a wicked woman, for out of the abundance of my complaint and grief I have spoken until now."

Then Eli answered and said, "Go in peace, and the God of Israel grant your petition which you have asked of Him."

And she said, "Let your maidservant find favor in your sight." So the woman went her way and ate, and her face was no longer sad.

—1 Samuel 1:12–18

AND THE LORD VISITED HANNAH

Do not be disappointed if people don't understand you as you're dealing with your trial. Merely be a child of your Father in heaven, for He will always understand. Remember that Psalm 46:1 says, *"God is our refuge and strength, a very present help in trouble."*

It came to pass that the Lord visited Hannah, just like the servant of God had said, and she conceived and gave birth to a son she named Samuel, dedicating him to the Lord to be at His service all his life. From his childhood with Eli the priest, Samuel became a great prophet after Moses and the last judge in Israel. He remained faithful to the Lord's service all the days of his life.

And Elkanah knew Hannah his wife, and the Lord remembered her. So it came to pass in the process of time that Hannah conceived and bore a son, and called his name Samuel, saying, "Because I have asked for him from the Lord."

—1 Samuel 1:19–20

There is nothing God cannot do. Remember, prayer works.

Hannah realized that she had nowhere else to go for help, because those around her couldn't comprehend what she was going through. God finally became her last refuge; she gave herself totally in trusting Him, leaning on Him, and God saw her through. Her prayer was answered.

Trust in God in the midst of your sorrow, in the midst of mockery. Trust Him when you feel alone and powerless. Remember the prayer of King Jehoshaphat:

> *O our God, will You not judge them? For we have no power against this great multitude that is coming against us; nor do we know what to do, but our eyes are upon You.*
>
> —2 Chronicles 20:12

It could be a situation that creates fear, stress, or anxiety. Such was the case of Jacob, who apprehended a possible anger from his brother Esau, who could have killed him in revenge when Jacob and his family were on their way home to the territory of his father. Remember that he went to God with assurance, reminding Him of His promises, knowing for sure that the Lord would always honour His Word:

> *Then Jacob said, "O God of my father Abraham and God of my father Isaac, the Lord who said to me, 'Return to your country and to your family, and I will deal well with you'... Deliver me, I pray, from the hand of my brother, from the hand of Esau; for I fear him, lest he come and attack me and the mother with the children."*
>
> —Genesis 32:9, 11

And the Lord delivered him and his family. His brother Esau embraced him warmly.

He can do the same for you. Keep your eyes upon the Lord and put your trust in Him. He will be with you and see you through. In the midst of your sorrow, in the midst of your affliction, call upon the Lord. He will hear your prayer and answer you.

Thank You, Lord Jesus. Amen!

chapter five

Prayer with a Little Faith

rayer is very important in the believer's life, but prayer without belief is a useless exercise. We cannot approach God without trusting in Him; that's why believing in Him, or having faith in Him, is more than necessary. In fact, how can we ask things from someone and expect to receive if at the same time we doubt his or her ability to give and satisfy? The Bible says that if we cannot come to God without doubting Him, we cannot please Him.

The book of Hebrews explains it clearly:

But without faith it is impossible to please Him, for he who comes to God must believe that He is, and that He is a rewarder of those who diligently seek Him.

—Hebrews 11:6

However, it is so familiar to go to church regularly, read the Bible, participate actively in church activities, and be present in almost all prayer meetings only to have great difficulty believing in God, leaning on Him, standing on His promises in times of trouble, and knowing that in such moments we can confidently pray, believing that He will hear us and be with us through it. For it is by faith that we receive from the Lord when we pray. And Jesus recommends having faith in God:

So Jesus answered and said to them, "Have faith in God... Therefore I say to you, whatever things you ask when you pray, believe that you receive them, and you will have them."

—Mark 11:22, 24

Faith is so important that Jesus came to that statement many times and in many places, demonstrating the effect of *active faith* in the lives of people who had an encounter with Him. Sometimes He congratulated them for having great faith, and other times He reproached them for their little faith. It once happened that Jesus was surprised to see people who had great difficulty believing.

Now He could do no mighty work there, except that He laid His hands on a few sick people and healed them. And He marveled because of their unbelief.

—Mark 6:5–6

Need for More Belief

Immediately the father of the child cried out and said with tears, "Lord, I believe; help my unbelief!"

—Mark 9:24

We have here a situation where the disciples of Jesus were approached by a man who had brought his son to be delivered, for he was demon-possessed. Since Jesus was absent at that moment, His disciples tried to cast out the evil spirit—but they couldn't. The Bible says that there was a dispute between the scribes and the disciples, for around them was a great multitude. I imagine that the atmosphere was intense.

When Jesus came back, He asked what had happened. Right on the spot, the man reported about his demon-possessed son that the disciples had been unable to deliver.

And wherever it seizes him, it throws him down; he foams at the mouth, gnashes his teeth, and becomes rigid. So I spoke to Your disciples, that they should cast it out, but they could not.

—Mark 9:18

These words provoked Jesus, who exclaimed: *"O faithless generation, how long shall I be with you? How long shall I bear with you?"* (Mark 9:19)

The next steps expose one of the real problems in a Christian's life about belief and faith, a problem we could simply summarize this way: "I believe, but I don't know if it can happen." This makes Mark 9:24—*"Lord, I believe; help my unbelief!"*—a subject of great debate among those who by their knowledge of Scripture can express ideas about the Word of God.

In large measure, the conclusion remains that people want to believe, but doubt oftentimes holds them back. So it happened that as Jesus continued to ask the father more details about the boy's condition, the man said to Jesus, *"But if You can do anything, have compassion on us and help us"* (Mark 9:22).

The way the man presented his request to the Master shows that he wasn't sure that Jesus would be able to set the boy free, or he didn't have enough conviction and trust to accept the reality that his son could be delivered. Therefore, Jesus didn't address him directly according to his demand; rather, Jesus pointed that it wasn't a matter of whether he could do something, but rather if the father could believe: *"If you can believe, all things are possible to him who believes"* (Mark 9:23).

The Bible says that the man cried out to Jesus in tears, *"Lord, I believe; help my unbelief!"* (Mark 9:24) Paraphrased, he's saying, "I believe, but my belief doesn't meet the genuineness of belief that you require. Therefore, please, Lord, help my unbelief! Otherwise, help me to willingly accept the truth that you can deliver him."

And Jesus rebuked the unclean spirit. He commanded it to come out of the young man and to enter him no more. Then the spirit came out of him (Mark 9:25–28).

It's very easy to say "I believe" and declare that we have faith when our situations are going well. But when we face challenges and our faith is tested, we forget that God always keeps His promises. Let us not be people of little faith, as Jesus reproached them so often. Remember, temptations will come, but God will see us through. Jesus says,

> *These things I have spoken to you, that in Me you may have peace. In the world you will have tribulation; but be of good cheer, I have overcome the world.*
>
> —John 16:33

If it ever happens that you find difficulty believing, like the father of the demon-possessed son, cry out to the Lord and ask Him to help your unbelief.

The Bible shows us that after a teaching of Jesus on offenses and forgiveness, the apostles, conscious of their limits as humans, asked Jesus to increase their faith: *"Increase our faith"* (Luke 17:5).

Finally, do your best to grow in your faith by reading and meditating on the Word of God regularly. Feed your inner being with testimonies of the prodigious deeds God has done, and remember to count the blessings you have already received from Him. Say to yourself, "If God heard my prayer in the past and helped me, He still can do it today. Indeed, He will do it." Let it be so for you in Jesus' name!

The Lord Acts in Weakness

So he said to Him, "O my Lord, how can I save Israel? Indeed my clan is the weakest in Manasseh, and I am the least in my father's house."

—Judges 6:15

In Judges 6–8, the Bible presents the story of Gideon, a young man who couldn't believe that God was with the Israelites because of the calamities and oppressions they had suffered at the hand of their enemies.

One day, an angel of the Lord appeared to him, greeting him, *"The Lord is with you, you mighty man of valor!"* (Judges 6:12) See how the rest of the story unfolds.

Gideon said to Him, "O my lord, if the Lord is with us, why then has all this happened to us? And where are all His miracles which our fathers told us about, saying, 'Did not the Lord bring us up from Egypt?' But now the Lord has forsaken us and delivered us into the hands of the Midianites."

Then the Lord turned to him and said, "Go in this might of yours, and you shall save Israel from the hand of the Midianites. Have I not sent you?"

So he said to Him, "O my Lord, how can I save Israel? Indeed my clan is the weakest in Manasseh, and I am the least in my father's house."

And the Lord said to him, "Surely I will be with you, and you shall defeat the Midianites as one man."

Then he said to Him, "If now I have found favor in Your sight, then show me a sign that it is You who talk with me. Do not depart from here, I pray, until I come to You and bring out my offering and set it before You."

And He said, "I will wait until you come back."

—Judges 6:13–18

Then Gideon went and prepared the offering as he required it. When everything was ready, he brought the offering back and set it on a rock, as the angel indicated to him. The angel touched the offering with the end of his staff and fire came out of the rock, consuming it. Then the angel disappeared.

Now Gideon perceived that He was the Angel of the Lord. So Gideon said, "Alas, O Lord God! For I have seen the Angel of the Lord face to face."

Then the Lord said to him, "Peace be with you; do not fear, you shall not die."

—Judges 6:22–23

We can learn many lessons from this dialogue between Gideon and the angel of the Lord. First of all, we could say that Gideon's faith was influenced by his circumstances.

DOUBT, A DESTRUCTIVE WEAPON

At the beginning, he refused to accept that he was a mighty man of valour; he didn't believe that God was with the Israelites. If He was, where were all those miracles he'd heard about that had happened in the past? He couldn't believe that God was able to do anything, even to choose him to deliver Israel.

It's amazing to see the extent to which worrying about our problems can blind us from seeing that God has the solution. We forget that He is the Creator.

Gideon complained that the nation hadn't been delivered from the Midianites, but the Lord said to him, "Go out and save Israel." Instead of accepting, he presented God with many excuses to show his weakness, as if the Lord didn't know him. Is that not what the majority of us would do? When God charged Moses to go to Pharaoh in Egypt and deliver His people, Moses gave Him so many reasons why he couldn't do it. God showed him signs and prodigious works that no human could perform, but Moses kept refusing.

> *Then Moses said to the Lord, "O my Lord, I am not eloquent, neither before nor since You have spoken to Your servant; but I am slow of speech and slow of tongue."*
>
> *So the Lord said to him, "Who has made man's mouth? Or who makes the mute, the deaf, the seeing, or the blind? Have not I, the Lord? Now therefore, go, and I will be with your mouth and teach you what you shall say."*
>
> *But he said, "O my Lord, please send by the hand of whomever else You may send."*
>
> —Exodus 4:10–13

But our God is a great and good God. Many times we are slow to believe, and we are of little faith, but to demonstrate His great love He shows Himself to be patient and merciful. The strength of God is perfect in our weakness, and therefore He helped Moses by sending him his brother Aaron to assist him.

GIDEON ASKED FOR A SIGN FROM GOD

After Gideon realized for certain that God had indeed visited him through His angel, he was afraid that he might die from having seen the angel face to face. After receiving assurance from God that all was well, he worshiped the Lord.

Next, the Bible says that the enemies of Israel gathered together to attack, and Gideon by the Spirit of God stood up for the cause of the Lord. The Israelites responded from different tribes, following him into battle.

Then all the Midianites and Amalekites, the people of the East, gathered together; and they crossed over and encamped in the Valley of Jezreel. But the Spirit of the Lord came upon Gideon; then he blew the trumpet, and the Abiezrites gathered behind him. And he sent messengers throughout all Manasseh, who also gathered behind him. He also sent messengers to Asher, Zebulun, and Naphtali; and they came up to meet them.

—Judges 6:33–35

But before moving further, Gideon asked God for a sign:

So Gideon said to God, "If You will save Israel by my hand as You have said—look, I shall put a fleece of wool on the threshing floor; if there is dew on the fleece only, and it is dry on all the ground, then I shall know that You will save Israel by my hand, as You have said."

And it was so. When he rose early the next morning and squeezed the fleece together, he wrung the dew out of the fleece, a bowlful of water.

Then Gideon said to God, "Do not be angry with me, but let me speak just once more: Let me test, I pray, just once more with the fleece; let it now be dry only on the fleece, but on all the ground let there be dew."

And God did so that night. It was dry on the fleece only, but there was dew on all the ground.

—Judges 6:36–40

It's admirable to see how far God can go to show us who He really is. What a great example of patience and love!

In the case of Gideon, I don't want to say that he ever didn't trust in God, but I think that he wanted to be more thoroughly convinced. Not only had God said that Gideon would be the one to save Israel, but he now had to believe for himself that God wanted him to be the one to go ahead and do it. And God would guarantee his victory!

Sometimes we need more from God before we finally move. The importance of the cause requires us to be sure that we'll succeed before jumping in, and the only way to be sure is to know and believe that God's promises are indeed our guarantee. We must learn to take God at His Word and act upon it. That's faith, which requires total obedience—and God loves obedience. If God says so, well... it is so. If God says go, we must go. Otherwise we're not obeying Him. However, the Lord is patient with those who don't understand at once and ask for more light. He'll be patient because He sees our heart. He knows us, and He loves us. He loves all.

Gideon was conscious of his limits and weaknesses, so he didn't shut out all possibilities for God to enter his life and use him. This led him to ask God to demonstrate more of Himself, and God did. Finally he became convinced and his faith grew considerably, and the Lord used him mightily. He delivered His people from the hand of the enemies with God's assistance and all the glory went to the Lord, for God's *"strength is made perfect in weakness"* (2 Corinthians 12:9).

Don't let your little faith close the door to God, who would so much like to visit you! Move forward confidently with Jesus who is in you, because you can do all things through Christ who strengthens you (Philippians 4:13).

chapter six

Prayer to Seek God's Favour After Wrongdoing

The Word of God says that *"all have sinned and fall short of the glory of God"* (Romans 3:23). The fall didn't just happen today. Right from the beginning, the first man and woman on earth sinned by disobeying God's command. Since then, all creation has been defiled and corrupted. Sin then became our inheritance, our nature as human beings. In this sinful state, our ways, thoughts, and actions happen to be opposite to God's, and our perversity causes us to be condemned in His sight. Sin has covered the world with injustice, immorality, evildoings, and hatred. All the past ages of human history testify to this.

The firstborn son of the first man, Cain, killed his brother in jealousy. Afterward, we can see that the heart of humanity keeps progressing toward evil. Therefore, God became grieved in His heart about it:

> *Then the Lord saw that the wickedness of man was great in the earth, and that every intent of the thoughts of his heart was only evil continually. And the Lord was sorry that He had made man on the earth, and He was grieved in His heart.*
>
> —Genesis 6:5–6

The Word of God continues this way:

Therefore, just as through one man sin entered the world, and death through sin, and thus death spread to all men, because all sinned...

—Romans 5:12

But the Lord has always wanted us to choose to do good so that we won't have to pay sin's consequences. In fact, He doesn't want us to die because of our sins, but to live and have life forever with Him.

So the Lord said to Cain, "Why are you angry? And why has your countenance fallen? If you do well, will you not be accepted? And if you do not do well, sin lies at the door. And its desire is for you, but you should rule over it."

—Genesis 4:6–7

Later, the Lord added,

Do I have any pleasure at all that the wicked should die?" says the Lord God, "and not that he should turn from his ways and live?"

—Ezekiel 18:23

He also said,

Let the wicked forsake his way, and the unrighteous man his thoughts; let him return to the Lord, and He will have mercy on him; and to our God, for He will abundantly pardon.

—Isaiah 55:7

In the time of Noah, God destroyed the earth, including humans, because they were so evil in His sight:

And God said to Noah, "The end of all flesh has come before Me, for the earth is filled with violence through them; and behold, I will destroy them with the earth."

—Genesis 6:13

But the same God will abundantly pardon us, as we read above in the book of Isaiah.

For the wages of sin is death, but the gift of God is eternal life in Christ Jesus our Lord.

—Romans 6:23

The Bible keeps a record of many people who found themselves, at one time or another, sinning against God. After realizing their transgressions, they repented and asked for forgiveness. Let us be inspired from the experiences of a few of them.

Repentance of Heart

Against You, You only, have I sinned, and done this evil in Your sight...

—Psalm 51:4

Whenever someone offends God by not doing what should be done according to God's Word—whenever someone thinks, speaks, or acts in ways that express disobedience to God's command, and whenever we treat others contrary to God's will—we have sinned (1 John 3:4). Sin is transgressing God's Law. But because we are weak in our flesh (our sinful nature), we cannot by ourselves, by our own human efforts, keep doing what is good unless we stay connected to heaven. In the light of the New Testament, if we walk according to the Holy Spirit and are led by the power of the Spirit of God, we will not be submitted to our sinful nature.

I say then: Walk in the Spirit, and you shall not fulfill the lust of the flesh.

—Galatians 5:16

Jesus Christ says in John 15:5, *"for without Me you can do nothing."*

KING DAVID'S SIN

One of the tragedies of the Old Testament is the fall of King David with Bathsheba, the wife of Uriah, one of the mighty men in the king's army who was killed at his command. This account teaches us to always be careful and alert. The adversary is still misleading people today, the same way he tricked Eve in the Garden of Eden, dragging them into sin to destroy them and causing chaos in their relationship with the Lord.

Be sober, be vigilant; because your adversary the devil walks about like a roaring lion, seeking whom he may devour. Resist him, steadfast in the faith...

—1 Peter 5:8

The Holy Spirit adds this:

But each one is tempted when he is drawn away by his own desires and enticed. Then, when desire has conceived, it gives birth to sin; and sin, when it is full-grown, brings forth death.

—James 1:14–15

In the spring, a time when kings commonly went out to battle, King David sent out his army under the authority of his captain, Joab. David himself remained in Jerusalem. One evening, as the king was taking a walk on the roof of his house, he saw a beautiful woman, Bathsheba, taking a bath. Intrigued, he gathered information about her and sent his personnel to bring the woman to him; from there, he fell into immoral sin with her. Bathsheba became pregnant.

But it so happened that she had a husband, Uriah, who was a soldier in the king's army. In fact, Uriah was on the battlefield that very moment. David, trying to cover up his sin, invited the husband to return home, expecting that he would sleep with his wife. But the plan didn't work.

> *And Uriah said to David, "The ark and Israel and Judah are dwelling in tents, and my lord Joab and the servants of my lord are encamped in the open fields. Shall I then go to my house to eat and drink, and to lie with my wife? As you live, and as your soul lives, I will not do this thing."*
>
> —2 Samuel 11:11

Having failed in his plan, King David sent Uriah back to the battlefield with the recommendation for Joab to make his death possible.

> *And he wrote in the letter, saying, "Set Uriah in the forefront of the hottest battle, and retreat from him, that he may be struck down and die."*
>
> —2 Samuel 11:15

The reality is that the same devil who has presented us occasions to sin, because we've given him access to do so during our moments of weakness, will be the first to laugh at us when we face the regrettable consequences. How tragic is the disastrous effect of our sin on the relationship we enjoyed so well with God before we fell! Sin inflicts so much spiritual damage on us, and causes many people to be affected and disappointed in us.

DAVID FACING GOD

Now, what David did so displeased God that He was very angry against him. The Lord sent Nathan the prophet to the king with a parable that demonstrated the gravity of David's acts in the sight of God.

The parable was about a socioeconomically privileged man who had a lot of flocks. One day when a friend visited him, the rich man took the only little lamb a poor man had, and prepared it to receive his guest.

When King David listened to the prophet Nathan, he was so angry about the rich man in the parable that he pronounced a death sentence on his life for the cruelty of the sin he had committed.

> So David's anger was greatly aroused against the man, and he said to Nathan, "As the Lord lives, the man who has done this shall surely die! And he shall restore fourfold for the lamb, because he did this thing and because he had no pity."
>
> —2 Samuel 12:5–6

What David didn't realize was that Nathan had been talking about David himself and his evil deeds. You can imagine the intensity of the moment when Nathan said to the king, "You are the man!"

With reproach and bitterness, God addressed David through His prophet in terms that described a disgusting atrocity. The parable is now there to remind us daily of the heavy price we pay for letting sin overpower us. We must avoid sin at all costs as much as possible, with the Lord's help.

Let us read the direct Word of God to David through Nathan the prophet:

> *"Why have you despised the commandment of the Lord, to do evil in His sight? You have killed Uriah the Hittite with the sword; you have taken his wife to be your wife, and have killed him with the sword of the people of Ammon. Now therefore, the sword shall never depart from your house, because you have despised Me, and have taken the wife of Uriah the Hittite to be your wife." Thus says the Lord: "Behold, I will raise up adversity against you from your own house."*
>
> —2 Samuel 12:9–11

THE WAY OF FORGIVENESS

To King David, it probably only took one second of looking down from the roof of his house to lead him to put the stability of all his people, his family, his throne, his position as king, his relationship with God, and even his life in terrible danger. Generally, there are two attitudes people demonstrate when they're reproved for doing wrong: either they're upset because of pride and refuse to consent or they acknowledge their fault and submit. The Bible says that immediately after Nathan stopped speaking, King David humbled himself and confessed that he had done wrong in God's sight.

> *So David said to Nathan, "I have sinned against the Lord."*
>
> —2 Samuel 12:13

As king, David could have easily been led by the blindness of his status and given in to pride and arrogance, unable to recognize the authority of God through Nathan the prophet. But praise God that he still had the fear of the Lord hidden deep inside his heart, even though he had already messed up. Our Lord, who is merciful God, took note of David's humility and spared his life. But the verdict remained in effect.

And Nathan said to David, "The Lord also has put away your sin; you shall not die. However, because by this deed you have given great occasion to the enemies of the Lord to blaspheme, the child also who is born to you shall surely die."

—2 Samuel 12:13–14

The Word that goes forth from the mouth of God shall not return to Him void; it shall accomplish the Lord's purpose. So King David started to experience the wrath of God immediately, according to the word of the Prophet. Indeed, the Lord rose up adversity against him from his own house. In a short while, the son born to him from Bathsheba died, for the Lord struck him. Many tragedies followed, from murder and cruel death among David's children to the time he fled from the conspiracy of Absalom his son, with the majority of people in his kingdom, to save his life (2 Samuel 13–15).

THE FEAR

The pain, shame, humiliation King David felt during those moments of trial were nothing compared to his fear of the absence of God's presence. It would have been worse for him to be separated from God and the harmony they had shared in the past. He feared losing forever the privilege of enjoying the Lord's fellowship.

The Bible says in 2 Samuel 15:13 that a messenger came to David, saying, *"The hearts of the men of Israel are with Absalom."* Hearing such a message in a normal time, David would have gone to inquire from the Lord what he should do; he would never decide anything without the consent of the Lord. Now he was overtaken by fear, panic overpowering him because God's fellowship wasn't there. That's what sin does first to us: it cuts us off from the Lord's companionship, the enjoyment of His presence, our confidence.

> *So David said to all his servants who were with him at Jerusalem, "Arise, and let us flee, or we shall not escape from Absalom. Make haste to depart, lest he overtake us suddenly and bring disaster upon us, and strike the city with the edge of the sword."*
>
> *...So David went up by the Ascent of the Mount of Olives, and wept as he went up; and he had his head covered and went barefoot. And all the people who were with him covered their heads and went up, weeping as they went up.*
>
> —2 Samuel 15:14, 30

RELY ON GOD'S MERCY

At that point, David had no other alternative but to lean on God's mercy and favour, to place himself in the compassionate hand of the Lord. It was his time to say, "Whether He accepts me again or not, whether He forgives me or not, He will be my Lord and my God. Without Him, I am totally lost. I will cry out to You, O Lord, and stay at your feet until I am no more." Let us feel the distress of David's heart at that moment:

> *Then the king said to Zadok, "Carry the ark of God back into the city. If I find favor in the eyes of the Lord, He will bring me back and show me both it and His dwelling place. But if He says thus: "I have no delight in you," here I am, let Him do to me as seems good to Him.*
>
> —2 Samuel 15:25–26

69

PRAYER OF DAVID

One of the most important steps, if not the first one, in circumstances like this is to open your broken heart, face to the ground, and sincerely pour out your soul to the Lord with the truth in your mouth: "I have sinned against You, Lord. I offended You." So it was for King David, who in the climax of his calamity expressed himself frankly to God. He considered that the Lord had always been, and still is, merciful and righteous. Here are a few lines of his prayer:

> *Have mercy upon me, O God, according to Your lovingkindness; according to the multitude of Your tender mercies, blot out my transgressions. Wash me thoroughly from my iniquity, and cleanse me from my sin.*
>
> *For I acknowledge my transgressions, and my sin is always before me. Against You, You only, have I sinned, and done this evil in Your sight—that You may be found just when You speak, and blameless when You judge.*
>
> —Psalm 51:1–4

In this first part of the prayer, David presented himself before the judgment seat of the Lord as guilty, someone who deserved punishment. At the same time, he trusted in God's compassion to change his situation and cleanse him from his sin. He took all the blame on himself so that no one could reproach God for anything.

He then continued in a very important way: "I have inherited a sinful nature from birth, which means I cannot do what is good, what pleases You, O Lord. However, I understand that You want Your truth to dwell in the inner part of me, inside of heart. Lord, please clean me. Create in me someone new and bring back Your happiness into my life. Restore me to the state I was in before my fall and wipe away all my guilt. Then I will be pleasant to You and I will teach others how to walk in obedience to You. With great joy, I will praise and worship You again."

Purge me with hyssop, and I shall be clean; wash me, and I shall be whiter than snow. Make me hear joy and gladness, that the bones You have broken may rejoice. Hide Your face from my sins, and blot out all my iniquities.

Create in me a clean heart, O God, and renew a steadfast spirit within me. Do not cast me away from Your presence, and do not take Your Holy Spirit from me.

Restore to me the joy of Your salvation, and uphold me by Your generous Spirit. Then I will teach transgressors Your ways, and sinners shall be converted to You.

Deliver me from the guilt of bloodshed, O God, the God of my salvation, and my tongue shall sing aloud of Your righteousness.

—Psalm 51:7–14

God Forgave and Rescued David

The prayer of David was heard from heaven by the Lord, who granted to him favour and mercy. David's sins were forgiven, for he had acknowledged his transgressions in God's sight, and his life was restored. The Lord brought him back to Jerusalem, his fellowship with God was re-established, and he once again became king of the entire nation of Israel (2 Samuel 18–19).

Afterwards, King David expressed to God his happiness, the joy of his forgiveness, and his gratitude:

Blessed is he whose transgression is forgiven, whose sin is covered. Blessed is the man to whom the Lord does not impute iniquity, and in whose spirit there is no deceit.

When I kept silent, my bones grew old through my groaning all the day long. For day and night Your hand was heavy upon

*me; my vitality was turned into the drought of summer. Selah. I
acknowledged my sin to You, and my iniquity I have not hidden.
I said, "I will confess my transgressions to the Lord," and You
forgave the iniquity of my sin.*

—Psalm 32:1–5

We can easily understand from these verses the excitement
of King David, speaking to himself words of encouragement and
blessing the Lord for His goodness and mighty deeds. His mercy
is from everlasting to everlasting to those who fear Him, and His
righteousness extends to the children's children and to those who
remember His commandments and do them (Psalm 103:17–18).

Finally, with a heart full of gratitude, King David invites all,
wherever God has dominion, whether in heaven or on earth, to
bless the Lord.

*Bless the Lord, O my soul; and all that is within me, bless His
holy name! Bless the Lord, O my soul, and forget not all His ben-
efits: who forgives all your iniquities, who heals all your diseases...*

—Psalm 103:1–3

Maybe you've come to the conclusion that the wrong you've
done is so bad that God will never forgive you. Every time you
think about it, the same thought comes up to your mind: you cannot be forgiven. But let me introduce you to the One who created
you, who gave you your breath of life; He still keeps it in His hands.
Here is what the Bible says about the God of all living beings:

*Let the wicked forsake his way, and the unrighteous man his
thoughts; let him return to the Lord, and He will have mercy on
him; and to our God, for He will abundantly pardon.*

"For My thoughts are not your thoughts, nor are your ways My ways," says the Lord.

—Isaiah 55:7–8

As you can see, the Lord sends you a special invitation:

"Come now, and let us reason together," says the Lord, "though your sins are like scarlet, they shall be as white as snow; though they are red like crimson, they shall be as wool.

—Isaiah 1:18

Seize this opportunity and accept the loving hand of God, who wants to transform you into a new creature in Him. His Son, Jesus Christ, has paid for your sins by His death on the cross so that today, if you want it, you can have complete forgiveness and abundant life. All you have to do is give your life to God, and all your sins will be forgiven instantaneously. Would you like to try? If so, repeat after me this prayer:

Dear God, I am a sinner, and I'm so sorry for my wrongdoings. Please forgive me for all the bad things I have done in Your sight. I surrender myself to You now. Lord Jesus, I thank You for dying on the cross to pay the price of my sins. Wash me by Your blood and cleanse me totally. I give You my heart, my soul, my mind, my all. Save me through Your love and mercy. I am Yours. Thank You, Lord. In Your name, Jesus, I pray! Amen.

Remember: never let your wrongdoings prevent you from going to God as a child to his Father and asking forgiveness! But you must acknowledge your trespasses and plead before the Lord in a profound attitude of repentance. If you are sincere in your heart, He will see it and forgive you, as He did for David. We serve a merciful and just God. Thank You, Lord Jesus!

Let Me Die with the Philistines!

Then Samson called to the Lord, saying, "O Lord God, remember me, I pray! Strengthen me, I pray, just this once..."

—Judges 16:28

This is one of the saddest prayers in the Bible, from a human point of view, when we consider all the conditions surrounding it. The Bible says that Samson, chosen by God, was consecrated for His purpose even before he was conceived. According to the announcement of an angel of the Lord, he was to begin to deliver Israel out of the hand of the Philistines, who had kept them under bondage for forty years (Judges 13:1–5).

God gave Samson supernatural strength which he demonstrated throughout his many confrontations with the Philistines. But it seemed that the call of God over his life motivated Samson to choose his wives from among the Philistines rather than his own people. This produced more fights, quarrels, and disputes between him and the Philistines. A lot of Philistines had been killed by him, and according to the Bible God had His hand in it:

So he went up and told his father and mother, saying, "I have seen a woman in Timnah of the daughters of the Philistines; now therefore, get her for me as a wife."

Then his father and mother said to him, "Is there no woman among the daughters of your brethren, or among all my people, that you must go and get a wife from the uncircumcised Philistines?"

And Samson said to his father, "Get her for me, for she pleases me well."

But his father and mother did not know that it was of the Lord—that He was seeking an occasion to move against the Philistines. For at that time the Philistines had dominion over Israel.

—Judges 14:2–4

That relationship ended in a conflict which led Samson to his first battle with the Philistines, during which the Spirit of the Lord came upon him and he killed a thousand people (Judges 15). The Word of God says that Samson later took another woman from the Philistines as his wife, named Delilah (Judges 16).

Samson expressed great joy in taking revenge on the Philistines, as he used to say, *"With the jawbone of a donkey, heaps upon heaps, with the jawbone of a donkey I have slain a thousand men!"* (Judges 15:16)

SAMSON'S LAST PRAYER

Although it's true that Samson was interested in Philistine women by divine purpose, I'd like to believe he bore some responsibility in terms of choosing whose hands to place his heart into. After all, he had to be careful while in the midst of the enemy's territory. The truth is that his two Philistine wives didn't really care about his life. Did Samson have to trust them so far as to reveal the secret about his supernatural strength? God only knew.

So I am really sad about this last prayer of Samson, which seems to say, "The Lord sent me on a mission to destroy His enemies and deliver His people, but because of the type of wife I chose I found myself needing to pray for God to grant me the favour to die with my enemies."

Judges 16 tells us the sad adventure of the end of Samson's life. He was betrayed by his wife Delilah after unveiling to her the source of his strength, for she had been paid by the lords of the Philistines to enquire from Samson his secret. Samson gave her false answers the first three times, but the Bible says that he finally became so pressed by her, so trapped by her reproach, that he opened to her his heart:

> Then she said to him, "How can you say, 'I love you,' when your heart is not with me? You have mocked me these three times, and have not told me where your great strength lies."
>
> And it came to pass, when she pestered him daily with her words and pressed him, so that his soul was vexed to death, that he told her all his heart, and said to her, "No razor has ever come upon my head, for I have been a Nazirite to God from my mother's womb. If I am shaven, then my strength will leave me, and I shall become weak, and be like any other man."
>
> —Judges 16:15–17

She then promptly called a man to shave off the seven locks of his head, and afterward the Philistines who were hidden nearby came very quickly.

> And she said, "The Philistines are upon you, Samson!"
>
> So he awoke from his sleep, and said, "I will go out as before, at other times, and shake myself free!" But he did not know that the Lord had departed from him.
>
> Then the Philistines took him and put out his eyes, and brought him down to Gaza. They bound him with bronze fetters, and he became a grinder in the prison.
>
> —Judges 16:20–21

The lords of the Philistines later gathered to offer a great sacrifice to their god and celebrate, for it had delivered Samson, their terrible enemy, into their hands. They then sent for Samson from prison so they could make fun of him. They scorned him and covered him with mockery. About three thousand people were present in the temple of their god to rejoice. As Samson was in the middle of their ridicule, humiliation, and shame, he addressed to God a last prayer:

Then Samson called to the Lord, saying, "O Lord God, remember me, I pray! Strengthen me, I pray, just this once, O God, that I may with one blow take vengeance on the Philistines for my two eyes!"

—Judges 16:28

The Bible says that Samson took hold of the two pillars which supported the temple, bracing himself against them with one on his left and the other on his right.

Then Samson said, "Let me die with the Philistines!"
And he pushed with all his might, and the temple fell on the lords and all the people who were in it. So the dead that he killed at his death were more than he had killed in his life.

—Judges 16:30

The position Samson found himself in, overpowered by the enemies, couldn't be pleasant for any reader. First the Lord departed from him, and then the uncircumcised Philistines mocked him, he whom God had chosen.

When he prayed in great despair at the end, the Lord showed mercy and answered him, giving him back his strength one last time. Samson then died with his enemies, but the name of the Lord Almighty God was glorified anyway.

Finally, God is light and there is no darkness in Him. He hates sin but loves the sinner and wants to save him. To be saved, you must repent and come to him as you are, asking for forgiveness:

If we say that we have no sin, we deceive ourselves, and the truth is not in us. If we confess our sins, He is faithful and just to forgive us our sins and to cleanse us from all unrighteousness.

—1 John 1:8–9

He who covers his sins will not prosper, but whoever confesses and forsakes them will have mercy.

—Proverbs 28:13

May the Lord bless your reading. As the Word of God says, *"Keep your heart with all diligence, for out of it spring the issues of life"* (Proverbs 4:23).

Samson trusted in the security of his strength because it came from God, but he didn't know that the Lord could depart from him as he chose and acted foolishly. May his unfortunate experiences inspire us to watch over our decisions. Then our prayer will be a source of comfort for all.

chapter seven

Prayer for Our Persecutors

When we pray, it's very important that we not let anything become an obstacle between our communications and God. But it's even more important that we not let any offense deprive us of the right to pray for the person who has offended us. In fact, here's what the Bible says in the Gospel of Mark:

> *And whenever you stand praying, if you have anything against anyone, forgive him, that your Father in heaven may also forgive you your trespasses.*
>
> —Mark 11:25

GOD WANTS US TO LOVE THEM

Because a persecutor is someone who causes us pain, who torments or even terrorizes us, we aren't immediately motivated to pray for him or her with a pure heart. Our flesh, our sinful nature, doesn't let us forget the suffering we have endured. Therefore, our prayers for our oppressors don't express any sign of love. It's false, hypocritical.

However, as people of God and followers of Christ Jesus, we are called to show love to our enemies, to pray for those who persecute us. That's what identifies us as sons and daughters of our Father in heaven. If we really love God, if we love Jesus, we must love those who hurt us; we must love our enemies. It may not be easy at first, but God gives us the ability to do so when we want to obey Him in all things. Here's what Jesus said of this matter:

But I say to you, love your enemies, bless those who curse you, do good to those who hate you, and pray for those who spitefully use you and persecute you, that you may be sons of your Father in heaven; for He makes His sun rise on the evil and on the good, and sends rain on the just and on the unjust.

—Matthew 5:44–45

A child of God who walks in the way of the Lord, led by the Holy Spirit of God, will never be able to retaliate or take revenge; the Spirit of God in him will not allow him to do so. In fact, he will be in pain for his persecutors, for he will understand that their evil acts toward him occur because they don't know the Lord. This is what happened in the Book of Acts when the religious leaders couldn't suffer the word of Stephen, a man filled with the Holy Spirit. They stoned him to death, but he couldn't hate them; instead he prayed for them.

And they stoned Stephen as he was calling on God and saying, "Lord Jesus, receive my spirit." Then he knelt down and cried out with a loud voice, "Lord, do not charge them with this sin." And when he had said this, he fell asleep.

—Acts 7:59–60

The most memorable prayer of forgiveness has remained the one Jesus Christ spoke with deep love on the cross at the moment of His crucifixion. There, nailed between two criminals, He pleaded in favour of those who wanted His death: *"Father, forgive them, for they do not know what they do"* (Luke 23:34). What a merciful Saviour!

Whether in the New or Old Testament, whenever God's presence exists in a person's life, circumstances cannot prevent him or her from loving others and showing the love of God.

We Have Done Foolishly

Has the Lord indeed spoken only through Moses? Has He not spoken through us also?

—Numbers 12:2

While wandering the wilderness, Moses was required by his brother and sister to intercede before God on their behalf because they had both behaved wrongly toward him. The Bible tells us that Miriam and Aaron spoke against their brother (Numbers 12:1). It seems that jealousy may have been the motive for their dissension. They made the point that Moses wasn't the only person God spoke through; He spoke through them as well. This statement displeased God, who immediately called them and their brother Moses for a meeting.

> *So they said, "Has the Lord indeed spoken only through Moses? Has He not spoken through us also?" And the Lord heard it...*
>
> *Suddenly the Lord said to Moses, Aaron, and Miriam, "Come out, you three, to the tabernacle of meeting!" So the three came out. Then the Lord came down in the pillar of cloud and stood in the door of the tabernacle, and called Aaron and Miriam. And they both went forward.*
>
> —Numbers 12:2, 4–5

In very direct terms, God emphasized for them the difference between His relationship with Moses and His relationship with others.

"I speak with him face to face, even plainly, and not in dark sayings; and he sees the form of the Lord. Why then were you not afraid to speak against My servant Moses?"

So the anger of the Lord was aroused against them, and He departed.

—Numbers 12:8–9

Immediately after the Lord departed, Miriam became leprous and Aaron realized the gravity of their act of foolishness. Not only that, he realized how offended the Lord had been. Therefore, he begged Moses to forgive them and to plead in their favour before the Lord:

So Aaron said to Moses, "Oh, my lord! Please do not lay this sin on us, in which we have done foolishly and in which we have sinned. Please do not let her be as one dead, whose flesh is half consumed..."

—Numbers 12:11–12

MOSES PLEADED ON THEIR BEHALF

It would have been easy for Moses to say, "You wanted to trouble me, but God took my defence." Or he could have said, "If the Lord strikes you down, that means you deserve it. I am right in His sight. It is in all justice that you are suffering now. Since God has already settled the matter, I won't be involved in it."

But as a man of God and a responsible leader with a heart faithful to the Lord and to God's people, Moses listened to Aaron's request and pleaded with the Lord for the healing and forgiveness of his oppressors. The Bible says that God answered the prayer of His servant, but maintained the punishment of Miriam for several days. Afterwards, Miriam was healed from the leprosy and did not die.

So Moses cried out to the Lord, saying, "Please heal her, O God, I pray!"

Then the Lord said to Moses, "If her father had but spit in her face, would she not be shamed seven days? Let her be shut out of the camp seven days, and afterward she may be received again."

So Miriam was shut out of the camp seven days, and the people did not journey till Miriam was brought in again.

—Numbers 12:13–15

There are many lessons to be learned here. We have seen that those who are in a position of responsibility for the Lord, and who are devoted to their tasks, are very precious in His sight. We had better be careful about the way we treat them:

Obey those who rule over you, and be submissive, for they watch out for your souls, as those who must give account. Let them do so with joy and not with grief, for that would be unprofitable for you.

—Hebrews 13:17

Let us come back to the prayer. Again, remember that our offended hearts must not lead our behaviour or dictate our conduct, as we are to testify Jesus to others and demonstrate His love, particularly to those who have offended us. It is the will of God that we forgive others and pray for our offenders. God has forgiven us already, so we must forgive.

Oh Lord, help us to forgive those who have offended us, and to pray for them so that they may know you! Thank You, Lord.

chapter eight

Prayer to Choose According to God's Will

Choosing according to God's will is the wisest decision we can make. It prevents mistakes and allows us to avoid regrettable consequences. As human beings, we're often used to choosing quickly, particularly when we deal with emergencies or desperate situations. When we don't choose properly, we must live with disappointment and discomfort. How much more peaceful and secure it is when we know that God is aware of our choices!

The Bible records many circumstances which required good decisions, and the people involved understood the importance of acting with God's assistance. Let us have a closer look and make provisions for our own profit.

A Wife for Isaac

...He will send His angel before you, and you shall take a wife for my son from there.

—Genesis 24:7

Genesis 24 says that Abraham, becoming old, grew very concerned about the kind of woman that Isaac, his only son born from his wife Sarah, would marry. He didn't want Isaac to choose his wife among the daughters of the Canaanites, among whom they were living at the time, because those people didn't worship the true God, the Lord God of heaven.

While he was still alive, Abraham called his oldest servant, who governed his entire house, and made him swear that he would go to his family's country and there find a wife for Isaac. The servant obeyed and undertook the long journey; his faith was firm on the promise of his master that God's angel would lead him to the right place. It was very important for the servant to believe in Abraham's word and have faith that the God who had never failed his master would be with him in this adventure, for he didn't know anything about this country, nor the people he was supposed to meet there.

> *The Lord God of heaven, who took me from my father's house and from the land of my family, and who spoke to me and swore to me, saying, "To your descendants I give this land," He will send His angel before you, and you shall take a wife for my son from there.*
>
> —Genesis 24:7

PRAYER OF THE SERVANT

As the servant and his party pursued their journey, they reached a particular place where there was a well of water. Women usually came to draw water, and it was evening. The servant decided to address to God with this very meaningful prayer:

> *O Lord God of my master Abraham, please give me success this day, and show kindness to my master Abraham. Behold, here I stand by the well of water, and the daughters of the men of the city are coming out to draw water. Now let it be that the young woman to whom I say, "Please let down your pitcher that I may drink," and she says, "Drink, and I will also give your camels a*

drink"—let her be the one You have appointed for Your servant Isaac. And by this I will know that You have shown kindness to my master.

—Genesis 24:12–14

GOD'S ANSWER

It is very clear that this formulation of prayer had been suggested to the servant by the Spirit of God Himself, for the Holy Spirit helps us when we don't know what to say (Romans 8:27–28). This is a profound inspiration for us today. From the beginning of the prayer, we can feel the servant's devotion to Abraham; he didn't miss the opportunity to plead for God to show kindness toward his master.

His faith in God, submission, and total respect for Abraham and his interest brought great reward. He hadn't finished praying when a young lady came to draw water. According to his prayer, the servant asked her for some water to drink. Not only did she give him water, but she also did exactly as the servant requested in his prayer to God.

And the servant ran to meet her and said, "Please let me drink a little water from your pitcher."

So she said, "Drink, my lord." Then she quickly let her pitcher down to her hand, and gave him a drink. And when she had finished giving him a drink, she said, "I will draw water for your camels also, until they have finished drinking."

—Genesis 24:17–19

The servant kept silent to see if his entire prayer would be answered. Yes, she served water to all the animals. Then he gave her some presents to thank her and inquired about her parents. The servant was surprised when the young lady told him that she was the daughter of a relative of his master Abraham. She then invited him to her parents' home and presented him to the members of her family. At that point, the servant worshiped the Lord who had answered his prayer and shown kindness to his master by giving him success in his mission.

> *Then the man bowed down his head and worshiped the Lord. And he said, "Blessed be the Lord God of my master Abraham, who has not forsaken His mercy and His truth toward my master. As for me, being on the way, the Lord led me to the house of my master's brethren."*
>
> —Genesis 24:26–27

After being received by the woman's parents, and explaining to them all that the Lord had done—including the details of his mission, the reasons for it, and the way that the Lord God had faithfully accomplished it—the family blessed the young lady and let her leave with the servant to join her future husband Isaac, as Abraham wished it.

So Rebekah became the wife of Isaac. Nothing is impossible to God.

We have learned that we must believe, but above all we must always let God be involved first in our matter, for it will bring us success and God will be glorified.

The Holy Spirit had suggested that the servant present a petition before the Lord about the kind of lady he sought, for He knew that the man didn't have any idea of the type of person he was looking for to be Isaac's future wife. By faith, he respectfully submitted to God a proposition of demand; since his prayer demonstrated complete trust in God, and it would be for His glory, the request was granted.

As we are inspired from this servant's adventure and his faith in the Lord, let it be the same for us in our prayer lives day after day, in Jesus' name.

God Knows the Heart

And they cast their lots, and the lot fell on Matthias. And he was numbered with the eleven apostles.

—Acts 1:26

Because the Lord knows the hearts of all, including what we think even before the thought comes to our minds, it becomes advantageous for us to inquire from God about anyone we have to deal with, even before we do so. We must include God in our decision-making process, especially in matters regarding the kingdom of God, for the Bible says in Jeremiah 17 that God knows well the heart of men:

The heart is deceitful above all things, and desperately wicked; who can know it? I, the Lord, search the heart, I test the mind...

—Jeremiah 17:9–10

After Jesus ascended to heaven, the Bible says that the disciples went back to the upper room where they often gathered to pray together. Under the initiative of the apostle Peter, led by the Holy Spirit, they considered with whom to replace Judas, one of the twelve disciples who had killed himself after betraying the Saviour (Acts 1:15–26).

Two men, Joseph and Matthias, were proposed among those who were faithful witnesses of Jesus' ministry, accompanying Him everywhere from the time He was baptized to His resurrection.

From there, they agreed to pray to the Lord concerning the matter, so that God Himself would decide between the two men.

> *And they prayed and said, "You, O Lord, who know the hearts of all, show which of these two You have chosen to take part in this ministry and apostleship from which Judas by transgression fell, that he might go to his own place."*
>
> *And they cast their lots, and the lot fell on Matthias. And he was numbered with the eleven apostles.*
>
> —Acts 1:24–26

The Lord answered their prayer and chose Matthias to become one of the twelve, to be part of the great commission which is to proclaim everywhere the good news of the kingdom.

Let us not forget that God knows our hearts. Because of that, we cannot allow ourselves to choose in His place, or not to pray before choosing. Please, let the Lord direct your decisions. It will be for your blessing and benefit.

For a Right Successor

> *Take Joshua the son of Nun with you, a man in whom is the Spirit, and lay your hand on him.*
>
> —Numbers 27:18

For the sake of the cause, it is always profitable to choose according to God's will. Therefore, we respectfully salute those throughout the Bible who succeeded because they invited God into their decision-making processes.

In the particular case of Moses, he knew that the time had come to tear himself away from the head of the people of Israel, because God had pronounced it—although he would have liked to continue, and at least take a quick step into the Promised Land.

The Bible says that Moses was faithful in all the house of the Lord (Numbers 12:7). In fact, God had given to him a very serious task: to lead the congregation of the children of Israel from Egypt to Canaan, the land that the Lord had promised to their forefather, Abraham, as their permanent dwelling place. But they were impatient and didn't believe in God, complaining so much that they became the cause of a lot of pain to Moses. They brought sorrow and discouragement many times to his heart.

So Moses said to the Lord, "Why have You afflicted Your servant? And why have I not found favor in Your sight, that You have laid the burden of all these people on me? Did I conceive all these people? Did I beget them, that You should say to me, "Carry them in your bosom, as a guardian carries a nursing child," to the land which You swore to their fathers?

—Numbers 11:11–13

Their behaviour often disappointed God so much that He resolved to exterminate them:

Then the Lord said to Moses: "How long will these people reject Me? And how long will they not believe Me, with all the signs which I have performed among them? I will strike them with the pestilence and disinherit them, and I will make of you a nation greater and mightier than they."

—Numbers 14:11–12

But Moses quickly interceded for the people:

And Moses said to the Lord: "Then the Egyptians will hear it, for by Your might You brought these people up from among them... Now if You kill these people as one man, then the nations which have heard of Your fame will speak, saying, 'Because the Lord was not able to bring this people to the land which He swore to give them, therefore He killed them in the wilderness.'"

—Numbers 14:13, 15–16

Moses continued with a convicting plea on behalf of the congregation. The full speech can be read in Numbers 14, but here are a few pertinent verses:

And now, I pray, let the power of my Lord be great, just as You have spoken, saying, "'The Lord is longsuffering and abundant in mercy, forgiving iniquity and transgression."

—Numbers 14:17–18

As a true godly leader, not a selfish one who is thirsty for opportunities to have it all, instead of jumping on this offer of the Lord to make of him a greater nation by destroying those rebellious people who had disappointed Him so badly, Moses, with meekness, humbled himself in prayer, asking the Lord to forgive.

"Pardon the iniquity of this people, I pray, according to the greatness of Your mercy, just as You have forgiven this people, from Egypt even until now."
    Then the Lord said: "I have pardoned, according to your word."

—Numbers 14:19–20

A SUCCESSOR FOR MOSES

After that, the Bible says that the children of Israel continued to murmur and complain against Moses, contending with him as they pursued their journey, until the day when something happened which changed Moses' destiny forever (Numbers 20:1–13). As Christians, we must watch out for our tendencies to complain or murmur, which are signs of unbelief. The children of Israel offended God so many times along their trip to Canaan that they brought great bitterness to Moses. According to the Bible, they reached a place named Kadesh, but there was no water there. The people complained:

> *And why have you made us come up out of Egypt, to bring us to this evil place? It is not a place of grain or figs or vines or pomegranates; nor is there any water to drink.*
>
> —Numbers 20:5

As the people had done before, they contended with Moses, provoking him and revolting against him to the point that he became angry—so angry that he did the opposite of what the Lord had commanded him to do.

> *Then the Lord spoke to Moses, saying, "Take the rod; you and your brother Aaron gather the congregation together. Speak to the rock before their eyes, and it will yield its water; thus you shall bring water for them out of the rock, and give drink to the congregation and their animals."*
>
> *...And Moses and Aaron gathered the assembly together before the rock; and he said to them, "Hear now, you rebels! Must we bring water for you out of this rock?"*

Then Moses lifted his hand and struck the rock twice with his rod; and water came out abundantly, and the congregation and their animals drank.

—Numbers 20:7–8, 10–11

Because of that, Moses, the faithful servant in all the house of the Lord and patient in the sight of God, became disqualified from entering the Promised Land, for which he had worked so hard.

Then the Lord spoke to Moses and Aaron, "Because you did not believe Me, to hallow Me in the eyes of the children of Israel, therefore you shall not bring this assembly into the land which I have given them."

—Numbers 20:12

His soul yielded to disappointment, seducing him for a short time to be distracted from the focus of his life. Acting in the moment, he offended his God, whom he loved and respected so much, which cost him the fulfilment of his mission on earth.

A similar scenario had occurred in the past when the people had murmured about the lack of water. The Lord had asked Moses to strike the rock which would give water, and Moses had done so and water had flowed (Exodus 17:6).

But this time at Kadesh, God wanted to demonstrate His might and power in a special way to the congregation of Israel. He asked Moses to speak to the rock and water would come out. But Moses was so upset by their provocation that he struck the rock two times. Water came out of it anyway, but he hadn't followed the Lord's instruction.

At a later time, Moses begged God to let him at least cross the Jordan and see the land at a distance, but the Lord rebuked him severely and refused:

Then I pleaded with the Lord at that time, saying: "O Lord God... I pray, let me cross over and see the good land beyond the Jordan, those pleasant mountains, and Lebanon." But the Lord was angry with me on your account, and would not listen to me. So the Lord said to me: "Enough of that! Speak no more to Me of this matter."

—Deuteronomy 3:23–26

When the time came for Moses to depart for his eternal home, a new leader was needed for the congregation. Obediently, Moses addressed to God the request to choose someone:

Then Moses spoke to the Lord, saying: "Let the Lord, the God of the spirits of all flesh, set a man over the congregation, who may go out before them and go in before them, who may lead them out and bring them in, that the congregation of the Lord may not be like sheep which have no shepherd."

And the Lord said to Moses: "Take Joshua the son of Nun with you, a man in whom is the Spirit, and lay your hand on him; set him before Eleazar the priest and before all the congregation, and inaugurate him in their sight. And you shall give some of your authority to him, that all the congregation of the children of Israel may be obedient.

—Numbers 27:15–20

The Bible adds that Moses did as the Lord commanded him:

So Moses did as the Lord commanded him. He took Joshua and set him before Eleazar the priest and before all the congregation. And he laid his hands on him and inaugurated him, just as the Lord commanded by the hand of Moses.

—Numbers 27:22–23

It cannot have been easy for Moses to accept the fact that he had to leave his position of leadership just before entering the Promised Land, but he didn't let his disappointment hinder his godly character. He invited God to choose a leader for the congregation of Israel according to His will.

Truly, Moses wanted to continue, but above all he wanted to please and obey the Lord his God. That's why he asked God about a successor. The Lord answered him and chose Joshua, who successfully led the people of Israel into Canaan.

We can understand that praying for a successor may not be easy, particularly when it goes against our own interest. But as children of God, we must not act to satisfy our own flesh, our own desires; God's Word must come first in all circumstances. Let us allow Him to choose for us, and to influence our choices. Let God be pleased. If we let His name be glorified in all we do, we will see how peaceful our lives can be! So help us, Lord. Thank You, Jesus. Amen!

chapter nine

Prayer Seeking for What Is of Eternal Value

We are encouraged to pray, and by the grace of God a significant percentage of the body of Christ frequently responds. Whether the prayer comes in response to tragedies, times of need, or personal reasons, it remains clear that prayer still has its place in life.

While all things on earth are temporary, even those which are very costly, what belongs to God is eternal. So it becomes obvious that as human beings possessing a spirit and soul which are eternal, since God our Creator is eternal, we should, when we pray, seek first what is of eternal value, what pleases God.

But to do this we need to be sincere of heart, asking from God the grace to know His will and praying that the Holy Spirit will help us make it happen, for we will be required to forget ourselves and our own interests to make God and His interests our first priority. A majority of us are so familiar and attached to the things of this life that when it's the time for us to pray, we often just ask for possessions, materials, and that which can satisfy us personally in one way or another. But the Bible invites us to seek those things of above:

If then you were raised with Christ, seek those things which are above, where Christ is, sitting at the right hand of God. Set your mind on things above, not on things on the earth.

—Colossians 3:1–2

We usually place all kinds of demands on our prayers, but we gain more when we put the interests of the Lord first, even when our needs seem unbearable. Doing so is a sign that we trust God in everything, so we decide to submit all into His hands, whatever the outcome may be.

Solomon Asked for Wisdom

At Gibeon the Lord appeared to Solomon in a dream by night; and God said, "Ask! What shall I give you?"

—1 Kings 3:5

Regarding the matter of seeking things from above, we turn to the practical example of Solomon's prayer, in which he presented a special request to the Lord which has made history ever since.

SOLOMON'S REQUEST

The Bible says in 1 Kings 2–3 that the kingdom of God was established in the hand of Solomon. King Solomon loved the Lord and walked in the statutes of his father David. Therefore, the interests of the Lord were also his own interest. He wanted more to please God than to please himself.

That's why, when the Lord offered him the opportunity to ask for whatever pleased him, his request to God was totally different from what the majority of people would ask for in that circumstance. As a king, it should have been obvious that he would ask God for the security of his kingdom first, and then ask for riches and fame or the like. But the Bible says that Solomon required from the Lord an understanding heart so that he could lead the people of the Lord according to the will of God.

At Gibeon the Lord appeared to Solomon in a dream by night; and God said, "Ask! What shall I give you?"

And Solomon said: "You have shown great mercy to Your servant David my father, because he walked before You in truth, in righteousness, and in uprightness of heart with You; You have continued this great kindness for him, and You have given him a son to sit on his throne, as it is this day. Now, O Lord my God, You have made Your servant king instead of my father David, but I am a little child; I do not know how to go out or come in. And Your servant is in the midst of Your people whom You have chosen, a great people, too numerous to be numbered or counted. Therefore give to Your servant an understanding heart to judge Your people, that I may discern between good and evil. For who is able to judge this great people of Yours?"

—I Kings 3:5–9

The Bible adds that the words of Solomon pleased God.

GOD'S ANSWER TO SOLOMON

Then God said to him: "Because you have asked this thing, and have not asked long life for yourself, nor have asked riches for yourself, nor have asked the life of your enemies, but have asked for yourself understanding to discern justice, behold, I have done according to your words; see, I have given you a wise and under-standing heart, so that there has not been anyone like you before you, nor shall any like you arise after you."

—I Kings 3:11–12

We work times to meet our basic needs, but in the end the result is deceptive, because we often perform according to our own ways, trusting in our own abilities, efforts, and self-judgment. King Solomon was conscious of his limits as a human, his inability to meet God's standard, and his fragility to reign over the people of God adequately. Therefore, he went after the best from the Lord, not for himself but for pleasing his heavenly Creator. Because his own interest was absent in all that he asked God in his prayer, the Lord gave him all that he needed for leading the nation of the Lord. Moreover, he received an excellent bonus, something he hadn't asked for and which he couldn't have expected or imagined. The Lord said to Solomon:

> *And I have also given you what you have not asked: both riches and honor, so that there shall not be anyone like you among the kings all your days. So if you walk in My ways, to keep My statutes and My commandments, as your father David walked, then I will lengthen your days.*
>
> —1 Kings 3:13–14

Who wouldn't like to receive such a gift?

Solomon desired what was of eternal value, so he was rewarded above measure. He wanted to make God happy and the Lord gave him more joy and satisfaction and completeness than any other king before or after him.

Many have misbehaved because of fear or their inability to meet their earthly needs, and in so doing they miss the mark. Blessed was Solomon, who didn't focus on what he needed for himself but rather on what could bring joy to the Lord and comfort to His people. In so doing, he received more than anyone could ever expect.

I think this is the right time to quote Jesus Christ's words in Matthew 6:31–33:

> *Therefore do not worry, saying, "What shall we eat?" or "What shall we drink?" or "What shall we wear?" For after all these things the Gentiles seek. For your heavenly Father knows that you need all these things. But seek first the kingdom of God and His righteousness, and all these things shall be added to you.*

Not as I Will, But as You Will

My soul is exceedingly sorrowful, even to death. Stay here and watch with Me.

—Matthew 26:38

Here we experience the most painful and sorrowful prayer in the Bible, without exaggeration. It occurs during the agony of our Master, our Saviour Jesus Christ, at the Garden of Gethsemane, where His pain was so deep and unbearable that no one can imagine it.

He went to the garden with His disciples, then, accompanied by Peter, James and John, the Lord moved a bit further away to pray. He was much tormented. His soul was extremely troubled by the effect of our sins, the sin of the entire world which He was to carry on Himself alone, though He never committed any sin.

According to Luke 22:44, as He prayed more earnestly his sweat became like great drops of blood falling to the ground. To those three disciples close to Him, Jesus expressed that His soul was exceedingly sorrowful, even to death (Mark 14:34). It was there, at the climax of his bitter suffering, as he withdrew a stone's throw from the others, that He fell on His face and Jesus addressed a broken-hearted prayer to His Father. Let us feel Our Saviour's pain.

> *Then Jesus came with them to a place called Gethsemane, and said to the disciples, "Sit here while I go and pray over there." And He took with Him Peter and the two sons of Zebedee, and He began to be sorrowful and deeply distressed. Then He said to them, "My soul is exceedingly sorrowful, even to death. Stay here and watch with Me."*
>
> *He went a little farther and fell on His face, and prayed, saying, "O My Father, if it is possible, let this cup pass from Me; nevertheless, not as I will, but as You will."*
>
> —Matthew 26:36–39

JESUS' TOTAL OBEDIENCE

The weight of the atrocity of our iniquities required Jesus to address His prayer three times to His Father. Three times He asked God if He could avoid going to the cross. The Bible adds that it took an angel from heaven to come and minister to Him, giving Him greater strength (Luke 22:43). I presume that our iniquities were so repulsive that it was with great pain that He bore them. But He wanted to be obedient to His Father to the point of death (Philippians 2:8).

This was necessary because His death on the cross, to pay for our redemption, was the only sufficient solution for our salvation. His love for us and His obedience to His Father enabled Him, in the midst of His agony, to desire to please God His Father more than to consider his own pain. Therefore He said in the prayer, *"Nevertheless, not as I will, but as You will"* (Matthew 26:39). In so praying, Jesus was in agreement that the will of God must be done, that the plan of heaven must be accomplished.

The plan of heaven was the forgiveness of all sin, with salvation offered to all humankind.

Jesus was in the position to satisfy His own self, but He preferred to choose what was of eternal value. He had the power to accept or refuse to go to the end of His earthly mission, but He wanted what the Lord wanted rather than what He wanted for Himself (John 10:18). Because of that, you and I are saved today.

Let us imitate Him by looking for the interests of heaven above our own. As we seek more of what is of God, we will find ourselves spiritually dying to self, which means that we pay less attention to ourselves. The result will be that the harvest of the Lord becomes more abundant, and the Lord will be so happy!

Let us conclude with this advice of Jesus:

Most assuredly, I say to you, unless a grain of wheat falls into the ground and dies, it remains alone; but if it dies, it produces much grain.

—John 12:24

chapter ten
Necessity of Prayer

The importance of prayer in our relationship with the Creator makes it indispensable in our lives. We must commit ourselves to maintain a life of prayer continually. In fact, it is quite absolute that in His Word the Lord commends us to always pray, not only for us but for others also, and to do so in a way that addresses all aspects of life. Therefore, our hearts must open day and night to express to the Lord all varieties of prayer and wait patiently for an answer from heaven, which often brings relief, confidence, and comfort. Our cry will always be the same:

> *Give heed to the voice of my cry, my King and my God, for to You I will pray. My voice You shall hear in the morning, O Lord; in the morning I will direct it to You, and I will look up.*
> —Psalm 5:2–3

The morning expression of a heart in prayer declares, *"But to You I have cried out, O Lord, and in the morning my prayer comes before You"* (Psalm 88:13). Let us admire how our Lord and Saviour Jesus made His night profitable: *"Now it came to pass in those days that He went out to the mountain to pray, and continued all night in prayer to God"* (Luke 6:12).

And let us read a request of Nehemiah to the Lord:

I pray, Lord God of heaven, O great and awesome God, You who keep Your covenant and mercy with those who love You and observe Your commandments, please let Your ear be attentive and Your eyes open, that You may hear the prayer of Your servant which I pray before You now, day and night, for the children of Israel Your servants, and confess the sins of the children of Israel which we have sinned against You.

—Nehemiah 1:5–6

Prayer, like the Word of God, is a guarantee for our perpetual relationship with the Lord. In the same way, the Bible says about the Word:

This Book of the Law shall not depart from your mouth, but you shall meditate in it day and night, that you may observe to do according to all that is written in it.

—Joshua 1:8

Speaking of a blessed person who succeeds in everything, the Bible continues, *"But his delight is in the law of the Lord, and in His law he meditates day and night"* (Psalm 1:2).

PRAYING WITHOUT CEASING

1 Thessalonian 5:17 tells us that we are to *"pray without ceasing."* At first, many people hearing this verse will take it literally and ask themselves, "How could it be possible that somebody keeps praying without ceasing? This could give one a serious headache." But this refers to a conscious and permanent attitude of prayer, a lifestyle of continual conversation between two persons: us and God. It is developed progressively in our spirts and hearts, which are in much contact with the Holy Spirit through constant meditation of the Word of God. We receive from God's Spirit a

soft message, a whisper from inside that reminds us time after time to speak with God again and again and again. That's why we can continue to pray in our various activities—even while we're driving, controlling the car at the same time as we talk to God, with whom we are in a permanent and renewing fellowship, because His Word is hidden and ever-refreshing inside our hearts.

The book of Psalms gives us a close picture of what we're talking about:

When You said, "Seek My face," my heart said to You, "Your face, Lord, I will seek."
—Psalm 27:8

This is what happens as our hearts move into position to receive instructions from the Holy Spirit, who will remind us each day to pray, to express our thoughts to the Lord, and to do it once more, even though we don't say any word with our mouths. Finally, in our spirits we will be with God always. What a privilege! That's enough for us to be eternally grateful to the Lord.

So we could say, from a human point of view, that prayer without ceasing is like a bond, a deep tie between close friends in perpetual conversation. There will be no end to our prayers because of the continual work of the Holy Spirit. Prayer, like the Word of God, keeps us in constant mutual affection with the Lord so that we can delight in the enjoyment of His presence.

The result and advantage of this is greater than the meeting of our daily needs. It becomes our spiritual protection against the traps of the enemy, a security system when facing our own spiritual weaknesses. As we develop this life of constant prayer, meaning scriptural prayer which is fed by the Word of God, we will walk and keep walking victoriously with the Lord day by day. May it be so for you, in Jesus' name! Thank You, Lord.

All Kinds of Prayer

Because our need for prayer is enormous, God's purpose for us is to do prayer in all ways and for all people. No area of life is to be left untouched in prayer.

Life becomes more difficult and demanding over time. New challenges, types of sickness and disease, anxiety, depression, and stress take their toll. People are looking everywhere and by all means to know how to find peace and tranquillity, but who can give peace, real peace, and assure our restful security? In times like this, prayer is of great importance. Trust in the Lord in your time of need. Trust in Him in the midst of distress, in times of exhaustion, discouragement, fear, and loss of hope.

Through prayer, let us go to the Creator of our souls. Let us go to Him who brings comfort and tranquillity. Read what the Holy Spirit says to you through the Word of God:

> *Be anxious for nothing, but in everything by prayer and supplication, with thanksgiving, let your requests be made known to God; and the peace of God, which surpasses all understanding, will guard your hearts and minds through Christ Jesus.*
> —Philippians 4:6–7

The Bible tells us that God always listens when people pray. Therefore, all human beings will come to Him (Psalm 65:2).

But prayer is offered through many different terms. It could be a request, presenting a petition to God or asking Him directly, formulating a demand to Him. Other times it could be pleading before the Lord on another person's behalf, as Abraham did (Genesis 18), interceding and expressing with tears your concern. In yet other times, it could be to humble yourself in presenting a petition, then praying with supplication like Elijah. In other circumstances, it is to express gratitude toward God for what we have already received, and for what we are sure to obtain in the future, which is an act of faith. We even express prayers of thanksgiving for what the Lord refuses us, because we believe that He knows better than we do what is best for us.

PRAYER HAS POWER

Prayer works amazingly with power, as the Bible confirms. The prophet Elijah prayed that it might not rain, and it was so. Later, he prayed for the rain to come back, and it was so.

> *Elijah was a man with a nature like ours, and he prayed ear-nestly that it would not rain; and it did not rain on the land for three years and six months. And he prayed again, and the heav-en gave rain, and the earth produced its fruit.*
>
> —James 5:17–18

The believers prayed for boldness to preach the Word of God, and after that Peter and John were forbidden to speak in the name of Jesus.

> *And when they had prayed, the place where they were assembled together was shaken; and they were all filled with the Holy Spir-it, and they spoke the word of God with boldness.*
>
> —Acts 4:31

When Herod persecuted the first church, he put Peter in prison. But as the people prayed, an angel of the Lord came into the prison and set the apostle free.

> *Peter was therefore kept in prison, but constant prayer was of-fered to God for him by the church...*

Now behold, an angel of the Lord stood by him, and a light shone in the prison; and he struck Peter on the side and raised him up, saying, "Arise quickly!" And his chains fell off his hands. Then the angel said to him, "Gird yourself and tie on your sandals"; and so he did. And he said to him, "Put on your garment and follow me." So he went out and followed him

—Acts 12:5, 7–9

PRAYER FOR ALL PEOPLE

Therefore, we are all called to pray, and to pray for all people. We must pray for the body of Christ, for believers all over the world, and for those who stand on guard as leaders, elders in the house of God, intercessors, ministers of the Word. We must also pray for those who carry the Gospel of Jesus Christ to the ends of the earth, suffering all kinds of torment for the sake of the kingdom of God. We must pray for Christian families, for children, youth, and for those who are called to minister to them in the name of the Lord so that they might not be swallowed by the cruel traps of the adversary. Such was the exhortation of the apostle Paul to the brethren of Ephesus:

...praying always with all prayer and supplication in the Spirit, being watchful to this end with all perseverance and supplication for all the saints—and for me, that utterance may be given to me, that I may open my mouth boldly to make known the mystery of the gospel...

—Ephesians 6:18–19

We are also called to pray in cases of suffering and sickness.

Is anyone among you suffering? Let him pray. Is anyone cheerful? Let him sing psalms. Is anyone among you sick? Let him call for the elders of the church, and let them pray over him, anointing him with oil in the name of the Lord. And the prayer of faith will save the sick, and the Lord will raise him up. And if he has committed sins, he will be forgiven.

—James 5:13–15

It is the will of God that all human beings be reconciled with Him and obtain salvation for their souls, for all have sinned and have been, in fact, separated from God, their Creator, because of their sins. We all need a Saviour. Therefore, God has provided a salvation plan for us all in the gift of His Son Jesus Christ:

For God so loved the world that He gave His only begotten Son, that whoever believes in Him should not perish but have everlasting life. For God did not send His Son into the world to condemn the world, but that the world through Him might be saved.

—John 3:16–17

Many have already submitted their lives to the Lord, but a lot of people out there, in schools, workplaces, and in our neighbourhoods haven't yet reconsidered their position toward God their Creator and acknowledged Him as their Lord and God.

So we must pray that the God of all spirit and flesh will make a way for them to meet Him and that the Spirit of God will convince them to come back to the Creator of their souls, the maintainer of their breath of life. In praying this, we will help many more to reconcile with God.

Lastly, we must not neglect to pray for those who govern the earth, so that we may live in peace and continue to serve the Lord.

Therefore I exhort first of all that supplications, prayers, intercessions, and giving of thanks be made for all men, for kings and

*all who are in authority, that we may lead a quiet and peaceable
life in all godliness and reverence. For this is good and acceptable
in the sight of God our Savior, who desires all men to be saved
and to come to the knowledge of the truth.*

—1 Timothy 2:1–4

If by what you have read so far you feel that your life needs
to be rededicated to the Lord, or you would like to be reconciled
with God your Creator, let us pray together. Repeat with all your
heart this simple prayer:

*Lord God, I know that I am a sinner and need a Saviour. For-
give me my sins. Thank You for sending Your Son to die for me on
the cross. Lord Jesus, wash me by your precious blood. I surrender
my life to You, my Lord and my God. Please save my soul, and
right now I give You my all. Be my Lord and Saviour forever.
Thank You, Lord! In Jesus' name, amen.*

Congratulations! You are now in good standing with heaven.
What you have to do next is maintain a close relationship
with the Lord by reading the Bible regularly, with the help of the
Holy Spirit, and developing a permanent life of prayer. Talk to
God like you would talk to a friend. He will hear you and answer
you by His Spirit, a sweet little voice you will learn to hear from
the inside as you continue to read the Bible and pray.

Finally, find a living church where the teachings of the Word
of God are a priority and the love and compassion of Christ Jesus
is demonstrated in the life of the brethren, worshiping the Lord
through a sincere communion from a pure heart. May the Lord
help you, assist you, and bless you!

chapter eleven
Prayer with Perseverance

The Lord guarantees an answer to our prayers. That's why He invites us to pray always, and to do so steadfastly and consistently, even though, for reasons above our comprehension, answers may take more time to come or seem not to come.

> *...rejoicing in hope, patient in tribulation, continuing steadfastly in prayer.*
>
> —Romans 12:12

> *God is not a man, that He should lie...*
>
> —Numbers 23:19

What He has said, He has done it. The entire Bible can testify to this. Here's what the Lord says:

> *...if My people who are called by My name will humble themselves, and pray and seek My face, and turn from their wicked ways, then I will hear from heaven, and will forgive their sin and heal their land.*
>
> —2 Chronicles 7:14

This Word is true, and will remain true forever and ever. If we, as believers in God, decide to humble ourselves, acknowledge that we need the Lord, and cry to Him sincerely with a repentant heart, committing to please Him from that moment on and doing nothing but His will, God says, "I will hear from heaven, and will forgive your sin and heal your land." This means that our prayers today can be answered, as well can our sins be forgiven by God. Therefore, we must be sincere in our attitude, pray consistently, and be of a godly, appropriate heart. If we need to spend more time before the Lord, let us do it. Let our perseverance attract the attention of God.

DOES GOD REALLY ANSWER ALL PRAYER?

This book would miss its mark if it didn't allow this question to be asked, and I'm sure that many who have read this far are waiting for the answer. Does God really answer all prayer? The answer, without any doubt, is *yes*.

Are all the answers to prayer exactly what people expect, or exactly what people want to receive? The answer: possibly, but not necessarily.

In this regard, many people are disappointed and don't go to church anymore. Others become enemies to God, so bitter and frustrated that they won't allow the name of God to be spoken in their presence.

Recently, I approached one of my neighbours who was suffering from back pain. As we spoke, our conversation turned to God. The man suddenly became so tense.

"What happened?" I asked. "Why did you change?"

"I don't believe in those things anymore."

"You used to believe," I pointed out.

His answer was so furious: "If that God was really a God, how come all of us prayed so intensely for our sister, who died with cancer, and yet He let her die without answering our prayer?"

As I listened to him, and thought for a moment about all he had said, I realized that I have known many situations similar to his. I understand him. However, I'm sure that God understands him more, and He feels his pain also.

WHAT IS THE BEST FOR US?

The reality is that we know what we need and what we would like to have as human beings. For example, maybe we lack basic necessities. Therefore we pray accordingly, seeking an answer from God that will bring about a breakthrough or change in our situation. We think we know what we expect. But the real question is, what is the best thing for us at that moment?

To this, we as humans don't know. Only God knows what's best for us. So we know what we need, but God decides what is good, what is best for us, and the way we will possess it. God will give us what we want when what we want is in accord with what He wants for us. But when what we want is in conflict with what He wants for us, or what is good for us according to Him, He will give us the answer we don't expect.

We don't have any other choice but to stand on the testimony of the three young Hebrews Shadrach, Meshach, and Abednego. They said, *"[O]ur God whom we serve is able to deliver us... and He will deliver us"* (Daniel 3:17). In the very next verse, they added, and I paraphrase, "But if not, He will always remain Our God." In the same manner—through trials, afflictions, hardships, and times of great need—may our Lord always remain our God.

Finally, we must remember that God is able to give us everything good that we ask Him—but what He wants for us is what is good according to Him. Since the Lord knows us better than we know ourselves, what He decides concerning us is for our good, even though it may not seem that way. The Lord is always right.

As we seek comfort in Him through our discomfort, He will give us the strength and joy to continue and make a way with Him until we will celebrate together once and for all. In the meantime, let us enjoy a true testimony and learn more!

TRUE TESTIMONY

Some years ago, my family prayer team was asked to pray for a man who had contracted cancer. His family, who was very wealthy, belonged to another faith. They were professionals and highly qualified people. But he and his wife were Christians, and because of that their relationship with the man's family was unenthusiastic.

When we learned of their situation, the man had already been admitted to the hospital for treatment. His state was very critical. But we gave ourselves totally in prayer for him, and we encouraged his wife to believe that all things are possible with God. We made this situation our top priority and continued to plead seriously before the Lord without interruption. We all prayed with faith, standing on the promises of God and waiting for the great result, which was his healing.

Since we lived a long distance away, we couldn't hear news about him everyday, but we kept praying. We became so confident in our prayer that for us, without a doubt, the case was well settled.

Then we heard that the man had fallen into a coma. Right after that, his wife had to make the decision of whether to continue life support. We cried out to God, "No! Please, Lord, do not let this happen." We increased our prayer and our hope, for I had in mind that his kids would miss their father at a young age, and his wife already wasn't welcome among his family.

One night, I had a dream in which I saw someone in high authority bring me a file. I recognized that it was the file containing all our prayers addressed to God for this gentleman. The person in high authority said to me, in a majestic tone I could not contest, "You may close the file now!"

I was so sad, because I understood what it meant. I didn't want to close the file, but the authority of this person was supreme. With tears, I conceded and submitted, closing the file.

Then I woke up.

Two or three days later, we heard that a member of the sick man's family, a medical doctor, had decided it was best to unplug him. So they had done so, and he was gone.

My family and I felt like a great sports team that had lost an important match. For days, I continued to ask God about what more we should have done! We finally left it to Him. Frankly, I was sad, but God has His own way of doing things.

From the time this sick man had become a Christian, he had created different charity works in which he took care of people in poor communities in the inner core of the city where he lived, people who were financially disadvantaged. On the day of his funeral, his relatives were shocked to hear and see thousands of people arrive to testify to how their condition of life, and the lives of their families, had been transformed for better because of the love of this man.

As the man's relatives saw the magnitude, and the beauty of so many testimonies about the kindness and love of Christ producing so much fruit from his life, they all chose to give their lives to Jesus Christ.

What's fascinating here is that when the man was alive, he and his parents didn't have a good relationship because he had chosen to follow Jesus Christ. Now, during his funeral, they discovered the beauty of the love of Christ which had been in him. They accepted Jesus and became Christians. Is this not wonderful? Can we understand the deep mind of God?

This recalls the apostle Paul's exclamation in the book of Romans, when he said,

Oh, the depth of the riches both of the wisdom and knowledge of God! How unsearchable are His judgments and His ways past finding out!
"For who has known the mind of the Lord? Or who has become His counselor?"

—Romans 11:33–34

And let us never forget that, above all answers to prayer we could receive from the Lord, the best of the best is the salvation of our souls.

Should we then continue to pray and believe God for an answer that pleases us? Yes, because we need to trust God in what He has decided. But as we pray, and keep praying steadfastly with perseverance, let us believe in His Word and in each of His promises as it is written in the Bible, for the Word coming out of God's mouth shall not return to Him without accomplishing the purpose it was sent for (Isaiah 55:10–11).

ESTHER'S MIRACLE

The true story of my daughter Esther remains in my heart as one of the most wonderful souvenirs of what our great God can do.

On Saturday, March 1, 2003, I received a call from my wife to come back home very quickly. I asked myself along the way back what could have happened!

When I got home, the atmosphere was stressful. In a hurry, my wife explained that Esther, our two-year-old daughter, had fallen into sudden respiratory distress. As her situation worsened, my wife, who is a registered nurse, decided to call our city's children's hospital for advice. After speaking to the appropriate nurse, it was determined that this was a 911 emergency.

The nurse on the phone wanted to call an ambulance automatically, but we preferred to take our daughter to the hospital ourselves. The nurse was concerned about lack of oxygen in the car, so she explained to us how serious this was and the importance of having oxygen near us in the car during transport. As we hadn't experienced anything like this before, we underestimated the gravity of the situation.

With the assistance of my niece, we jumped promptly in the car and left at a high speed. While in the car, we realized what the nurse had tried to explain to us about the severity of Esther's condition. Our daughter tried to stretch herself up, fighting to breathe, so we opened the windows. We continued to pray, calling out to Jesus as we drove as fast as we could, until finally we got to the hospital by God's grace and assistance.

As soon as we reached the emergency room, the staff, having anticipated our arrival, admitted Esther to an observation room. Following a consultation, the respiratory specialist and the nurse agreed right away that Esther needed a bronchodilator, a mask, and an oxygen tent.

Despite all these treatments, there was no improvement over time. In fact, Esther was getting worst. It suddenly became a battle between life and death; her colour changed, her hair stood up, and seemed to be at her end.

In that moment, the nurse said to my wife, "Mum, she really needs you now."

We sat very close to her, watching as she fought for breath. The doctors and nurses looked on with sad expressions, powerless. She seemed to be struggling for her last breaths. All signs pointed to this being the end.

Throughout this ordeal, my wife and I held hands and prayed. As the medical staff lost all hope, we stood on the promises of God in the Bible, our only hope and strength. The situation remained critical, but we remained standing on God's promises through His absolute Word. There, we found hope.

This poor man cried out, and the Lord heard him, and saved him out of all his troubles. The angel of the Lord encamps all around those who fear Him, and delivers them.

—Psalm 34:6–7

No evil shall befall you, nor shall any plague come near your dwelling; for He shall give His angels charge over you, to keep you in all your ways...

"Because he has set his love upon Me, therefore I will deliver him; I will set him on high, because he has known My name. He shall call upon Me, and I will answer him; I will be with him in trouble; I will deliver him and honor him. With long life I will satisfy him, and show him My salvation."

—Psalm 91:10–11, 14–16

At that point, her breathing reached its worst, so they rushed her to the trauma room. As we kept praying, reminding God of His promises for His children, Jesus miraculously kept her alive.

Later, during the night, they transferred her to the intensive care unit. My wife, who spent all the night with her, continued to pray and asked God to show favour to the little one in the same way He does for others who testify of His goodness.

"O Lord, make today the day You will visit Esther for Your glory," she prayed.

On Sunday morning, Esther opened her eyes and said. "Mamie!"

With a beautiful smile! What a miracle! Praise the Lord.

That evening around 7:00 p.m., by the infinite grace of our loving, merciful God, she was transferred to a normal room. And two days later, Esther returned home, breathing freely without any wheezing.

Soon after, we went with her to her paediatrician, who confirmed that she was perfect. According to the hospital medical staff, this kind of breathing problem should have been caused by a well-known virus, but they ran all sorts of tests and couldn't find any trace of the virus. They looked for three other possible viruses that could be responsible, but again the tests were negative. The doctors were unable, in spite of their efforts, to explain the tragic situation.

But we thank God that He was present with us during that crucial experience. Even when Esther was struggling for breath, when all hope was lost, the name of Jesus sustained her. There is power in prayer.

Jesus still heals today, just as He used to do in the past, for He does not change. Just believe in the promises of God in the Bible.

Esther is now a beautiful and very healthy young girl who loves and serves the Lord faithfully. By God's grace, she is pursuing the fulfilment of her destiny. Thank You, Lord, for that wonderful miracle!

Conclusion

This book has been written for your inspiration, to give you a closer look at stories from the Bible in which men and women have made a remarkable difference through their prayers. I hope this book has helped provide you with a better understanding of how these men and women's state of heart, faith in the Lord, relationship with God, obedience to God's Word, and total dependence on the Lord played an important role in God's answer after their prayer. Through them and their experiences, we can be encouraged today and confidently pray whenever or wherever we face challenges, trials, and situations of great need which require us to seek the face of the Lord. Their examples can help to strengthen our own prayer lives.

May the Lord of all spirit and flesh, who has called us to pray and give ourselves to prayer steadfastly and diligently without ceasing, help us to do so in Jesus's name. Amen!

Thank You, Lord Jesus!

About the Author

Jordanis Joseph is a devoted servant and minister of the Lord who loves the ministry of prayer and the Word of God with all his heart. He and his wife Rose-Marie have six lovely children—Rebecca, Daniel, David, Elizabeth, Esther, and Rachel. They all love Jesus and serve Him sincerely, by His grace. They live in Ottawa, Ontario.

josephjordanis@hotmail.com
www.divinerestorationhouse.com